OPPOSING VIEWPOINTS® SERIES

Birth Control

Other Books of Related Interest:

Opposing Viewpoints Series
The Catholic Church
Global Sustainability
Sexual Assault on Campus
Teenage Sexuality

At Issue Series
The Affordable Care Act
Are Abortion Rights Threatened?
Polygamy
Sexual Assault and the Military

Current Controversies Series
Abortion
Medical Ethics
Politics and Religion
Violence Against Women

"Congress shall make no law . . . abridging the freedom of speech, or of the press."

First Amendment to the US Constitution

The basic foundation of our democracy is the First Amendment guarantee of freedom of expression. The Opposing Viewpoints series is dedicated to the concept of this basic freedom and the idea that it is more important to practice it than to enshrine it.

OPPOSING VIEWPOINTS® SERIES

Birth Control

Jack Lasky, Book Editor

GREENHAVEN PRESS
A part of Gale, Cengage Learning

GALE
CENGAGE Learning·

Farmington Hills, Mich • San Francisco • New York • Waterville, Maine
Meriden, Conn • Mason, Ohio • Chicago

Judy Galens, *Manager, Frontlist Acquisitions*

© 2016 Greenhaven Press, a part of Gale, Cengage Learning.

Gale and Greenhaven Press are registered trademarks used herein under license.

For more information, contact:
Greenhaven Press
27500 Drake Rd.
Farmington Hills, MI 48331-3535
Or you can visit our Internet site at gale.cengage.com

Articles in Greenhaven Press anthologies are often edited for length to meet page requirements. In addition, original titles of these works are changed to clearly present the main thesis and to explicitly indicate the author's opinion. Every effort is made to ensure that Greenhaven Press accurately reflects the original intent of the authors. Every effort has been made to trace the owners of copyrighted material.

Cover Image copyright © Sebastian Kaulitzki/Shutterstock.com.

LIBRARY OF CONGRESS CATALOGING-IN-PUBLICATION DATA

Birth control / Jack Lasky, book editor.
    pages cm. -- (Opposing viewpoints)
Includes bibliographical references and index.
ISBN 978-0-7377-7506-8 (hardcover) -- ISBN 978-0-7377-7507-5 (pbk.)
1. Birth control. 2. Birth control--United States. I. Lasky, Jack.
HQ766.B4794 2016
363.9'60973--dc23
                        2015025016

Printed in the United States of America
    1 2 3 4 5   19 18 17 16 15

Contents

Chapter 3: What Concerns Does Birth Control Raise?

Why Consider Opposing Viewpoints?

> *"The only way in which a human being can make some approach to knowing the whole of a subject is by hearing what can be said about it by persons of every variety of opinion and studying all modes in which it can be looked at by every character of mind. No wise man ever acquired his wisdom in any mode but this."*
>
> *John Stuart Mill*

In our media-intensive culture it is not difficult to find differing opinions. Thousands of newspapers and magazines and dozens of radio and television talk shows resound with differing points of view. The difficulty lies in deciding which opinion to agree with and which "experts" seem the most credible. The more inundated we become with differing opinions and claims, the more essential it is to hone critical reading and thinking skills to evaluate these ideas. Opposing Viewpoints books address this problem directly by presenting stimulating debates that can be used to enhance and teach these skills. The varied opinions contained in each book examine many different aspects of a single issue. While examining these conveniently edited opposing views, readers can develop critical thinking skills such as the ability to compare and contrast authors' credibility, facts, argumentation styles, use of persuasive techniques, and other stylistic tools. In short, the Opposing Viewpoints Series is an ideal way to attain the higher-level thinking and reading skills so essential in a culture of diverse and contradictory opinions.

In addition to providing a tool for critical thinking, Opposing Viewpoints books challenge readers to question their own strongly held opinions and assumptions. Most people form their opinions on the basis of upbringing, peer pressure, and personal, cultural, or professional bias. By reading carefully balanced opposing views, readers must directly confront new ideas as well as the opinions of those with whom they disagree. This is not to argue simplistically that everyone who reads opposing views will—or should—change his or her opinion. Instead, the series enhances readers' understanding of their own views by encouraging confrontation with opposing ideas. Careful examination of others' views can lead to the readers' understanding of the logical inconsistencies in their own opinions, perspective on why they hold an opinion, and the consideration of the possibility that their opinion requires further evaluation.

Evaluating Other Opinions

To ensure that this type of examination occurs, Opposing Viewpoints books present all types of opinions. Prominent spokespeople on different sides of each issue as well as well-known professionals from many disciplines challenge the reader. An additional goal of the series is to provide a forum for other, less known, or even unpopular viewpoints. The opinion of an ordinary person who has had to make the decision to cut off life support from a terminally ill relative, for example, may be just as valuable and provide just as much insight as a medical ethicist's professional opinion. The editors have two additional purposes in including these less known views. One, the editors encourage readers to respect others' opinions—even when not enhanced by professional credibility. It is only by reading or listening to and objectively evaluating others' ideas that one can determine whether they are worthy of consideration. Two, the inclusion of such viewpoints encourages the important critical thinking skill of objectively evaluating an author's credentials and bias. This evaluation will illuminate an author's reasons for taking a particular stance on an issue and will aid in readers' evaluation of the author's ideas.

It is our hope that these books will give readers a deeper understanding of the issues debated and an appreciation of the complexity of even seemingly simple issues when good and honest people disagree. This awareness is particularly important in a democratic society such as ours in which people enter into public debate to determine the common good. Those with whom one disagrees should not be regarded as enemies but rather as people whose views deserve careful examination and may shed light on one's own.

Thomas Jefferson once said that "difference of opinion leads to inquiry, and inquiry to truth." Jefferson, a broadly educated man, argued that "if a nation expects to be ignorant and free . . . it expects what never was and never will be." As individuals and as a nation, it is imperative that we consider the opinions of others and examine them with skill and discernment. The Opposing Viewpoints series is intended to help readers achieve this goal.

David L. Bender and Bruno Leone,
Founders

Introduction

"In the eyes of many religious Americans, contraception still appears to promote sin and interfere with the divine plan. To those who want contraception to be widely available, the religious opposition seems entirely irrelevant, especially in light of practical concerns about disease and poverty. The two positions remain entirely irreconcilable. Hence, . . . we're still having this conversation."

—Brian Resnick,
"The Decades-Old
Contraception Debate,"
Atlantic, March 9, 2012

Birth control, by definition, is understood to refer to any attempt to prevent a pregnancy from occurring as the result of sexual activity. Over the years, there have been many different forms and methods of birth control, both natural and artificial. Regardless of mechanism, all these approaches offer the same fundamental benefit of affording people greater control over their reproductive activities so that they can plan the spacing of births and the size of their families as they desire. Because many people, particularly those affiliated with various religious groups, object to the idea of birth control on moral grounds, however, it remains a controversial and hotly debated topic.

As a concept, birth control has existed since ancient times, when the earliest traditional and technological approaches to contraception were first developed. The first traditional forms of birth control included withdrawal and the type of fertility cycle prediction referred to today as the rhythm method.

Some of the first technological birth control methods, which involve the use of man-made devices designed to prevent conception, included lambskin condoms and tortoiseshell diaphragms. These were the first forms of birth control to be based on the premise of creating a physical barrier between sperm and egg. Over time, barrier methods such as these were refined and updated, with the first modern condoms and diaphragms appearing in the 1930s.

Three decades later, birth control technology took a major step forward with the introduction of hormonal birth control in the form of the birth control pill in the 1960s. Unlike barrier method contraceptives, the pill worked by delivering synthetic estrogen and other hormones into the female reproductive system so as to prevent ovulation from occurring in the first place. A short time later, the first modern intrauterine devices (IUDs) were developed. These devices, which are implanted directly into the uterus, were designed to prevent conception by killing or damaging the sperm or otherwise preventing it from reaching the uterus. Although its early incarnations were occasionally problematic, the IUD eventually gained recognition as one of the safest and most reliable long-term forms of birth control. More recent contraceptive innovations include updated iterations of the pill and IUD as well as alternative forms of hormonal birth control delivered via patches, rings, shots, and more.

Despite the growing popularity and increasingly widespread use of birth control, however, fervent opposition to the idea of artificial family planning still remains. Many religious and pro-life groups decry birth control as an immoral violation of natural law and religious teachings on the holiness of life.

Generally speaking, anti–birth control advocates view sexual intercourse as a sacred act that should be engaged in only for the purpose of procreation. As such, they regard birth control as an attempt to separate the responsibility of procreation from the sexual act and thereby promote casual, recreational sexual activity. Much religious opposition to birth control is also tied to abortion and whether the availability of contraception leads to more abortions or is itself a form of abortion.

In the 2010s, contraception became an especially heated topic in the United States because of the inclusion of a birth control coverage mandate in President Barack Obama's Patient Protection and Affordable Care Act health care reform legislation. While progressives and pro-choice activists lauded the inclusion of this mandate as a victory for women's reproductive health rights and an important step forward for American health care, the move ignited a legal firestorm. The mandate, which required most employers to cover the cost of birth control as part of their employee health insurance plans, was met with fierce opposition from business owners who were opposed to certain contraceptive methods on religious grounds. Eventually, the battle over the birth control mandate went all the way to the Supreme Court in *Burwell v. Hobby Lobby Stores Inc.*, a case that ultimately resulted in new exemptions for certain objecting businesses.

Opposing Viewpoints: Birth Control examines the often controversial topic of birth control in chapters titled "Who Should Have Access to Birth Control?," "How Does the Affordable Care Act Affect Birth Control?," "What Concerns Does Birth Control Raise?," and "What Are the Social Consequences of Using Birth Control?" Moving forward, the public discourse on the practical, moral, and social implications of birth control use is likely to be more relevant and important than ever before. This volume offers insight into this discussion from an array of different perspectives.

OPPOSING
VIEWPOINTS®
SERIES

Who Should Have Access to Birth Control?

Chapter Preface

Contraception has long been a controversial topic. Is contraception a beneficial and morally sound approach to reproductive health? Much time and energy has been expended in debate between advocates on both sides of this question. While some think that contraception is a responsible means of preventing unwanted pregnancies and the transmission of sexually transmitted diseases, others believe that its use represents an immoral sin against nature that cannot be tolerated. Over time, the former argument has predominantly won out, allowing contraceptive use to become more widespread than ever before. However, the debate still continues as contraceptive advocates work to make various forms of birth control even more widely available.

In recent years, pro-contraception advocates have focused much of their attention on attempting to get access to birth control classified as a basic human right. Perhaps their biggest success in that endeavor came in 2012, when the United Nations Population Fund released a statement declaring that access to birth control was indeed a basic human right. While this statement was in no way legally binding, it elicited a strong response from people on both sides of the issue. For supporters, the announcement represented a significant victory in the fight to ensure that women around the world have the opportunity to enjoy the best possible reproductive health care options. For critics, the statement was a wanton violation of religious rights. From their perspective, classifying contraception as a right and therefore requiring everyone to pay for it would be an egregious slight to those who reject the idea of birth control on religious grounds.

The question of classifying birth control as a right took center stage again in 2014, when the Supreme Court was forced to make a decision on the validity of the Patient Protection and Affordable Care Act's (PPACA's) birth control mandate. The mandate, which required most employers to cover the cost of birth control for their employees, drew the ire of businesses operated by religious owners who objected to the use of contraception. Believing the mandate violated their constitutional right to religious freedom, the owners of the Hobby Lobby chain of craft stores filed a lawsuit against the government that eventually went before the Supreme Court. Although the court sided with Hobby Lobby in its decision and ultimately forced a revision of the PPACA's guidelines regarding contraception, birth control advocates remained determined to one day ensure that all people have the right to readily accessible contraception.

While the debate over contraception's status as a human right continues to be a major social issue, other similar arguments about the accessibility of birth control also have arisen. Whether teenagers should have easy access to birth control and whether a male version of the birth control pill should be manufactured are just a few of the many issues addressed in the modern contraception conversation. The following chapter sheds light on some of these issues, offering viewpoints from a variety of perspectives.

> "Women's right to contraceptive infor-
> mation and services is, in fact, an ele-
> ment of a number of key basic human
> rights. . . . Not only is guaranteeing ac-
> cess to contraception an integral part of
> these rights, but it is also a means to
> securing their fulfilment."

Birth Control Should Be Considered a Human Right

Maria Pawlowska

In the following viewpoint, Maria Pawlowska argues that access to birth control should be considered a basic human right. Highlighting the potential benefits of freely available birth control and the risks associated with enforcing contraception restrictions, she contends that establishing birth control as something to which all women have a fundamental right is an absolute necessity. Pawlowska is a health care analyst and writer whose works on reproductive health have been published by such organizations as RH Reality Check and the Maternal Health Task Force.

As you read, consider the following questions:

1. According to Pawlowska, how is the availability of birth control tied to women's social status?

2. According to Pawlowska, why is ensuring the availability of birth control particularly important in the Global South?

3. According to Pawlowska, how would better access to birth control be beneficial for both women and their children?

M argaret Sanger, an American sex educator, nurse, and legendary birth control activist once said that *"No woman can call herself free who does not own and control her body. No woman can call herself free until she can choose consciously whether she will or will not be a mother."* Nowadays, these words are true as ever and encapsulate the main premise behind a recent joint publication by the UN [United Nations] Population Fund (UNPF) and the Center for Reproductive Rights (CRR)—that the right to contraception is a human right.

Contraception and Politics

Michele Bachmann's recent foray into damning a public HPV [human papillomavirus] vaccination program for potentially harming 'innocent girls' shows how much politicians can get away with when it comes to reproductive health. When have you last heard anyone complaining about polio vaccinations? Oh right, it's not a sexually transmitted disease. . . .

It would have probably been even worse today if not for the Programme of Action from the 1994 Cairo International Conference on Population and Development (tellingly rejected by the Vatican). This document was an important milestone in changing the perception about reproductive health which is no longer a shameful issue to be dealt with in secrecy, but an important public health concern and a domain in which states should work to improve their citizens' quality of life. Therefore, the current perception of the importance of contraceptives in particular and reproductive rights and health in general should not be taken for granted. Most governments nevertheless still hate mentioning anything that can be interpreted to even mildly refer to sex about as much as they dread the thought of having to raise taxes 6 months before a major election. However, the the Programme of Action has made its mark. Importantly, it was also the first to suggest that access to contraceptives is a human right.

You may be thinking, "What? I can't remember condoms and the pill being mentioned anywhere in the Universal Declaration of Human Rights (UDHR)?!" You're right—it isn't explicitly mentioned (in the UDHR at least). However, the issue is a little bit more complicated than that, but really pretty straightforward.

Let's deal with the more complicated things first (and not to worry, they really aren't that difficult to grasp). As I mentioned in my previous post, the UDHR is not the only 'UN-approved' human rights document out there. There are actually a number of declarations (non-binding) and covenants and conventions (binding) which are part of the human rights legal framework and include, for example, the International Covenant on Economic, Social and Cultural Rights (ICESCR) and the Convention on the Elimination of All Forms of Discrimination against Women (CEDAW). When stating that access to contraception is a human right, UNPF and CRR drew on all these documents and did not limit their analysis to the UDHR.

Birth Control as a Human Right

And now for the straightforward part, in which we will see that access to contraceptives really is a human right—one grounded in the basic principles behind the very notion of human rights. Women's right to contraceptive information and services is, in fact, an element of a number of key basic human rights such as the right to life, the right to the highest

The Need for the Right to Family Planning

Today, family planning is almost universally recognized as an intrinsic right, affirmed and upheld by many other human rights. Because it is a right, voluntary family planning should be available to all, not just the wealthy or otherwise privileged.

"By Choice, Not by Chance: Family Planning, Human Rights and Development," United Nations Population Fund, 2012.

attainable standard of health, the right to decide the number and spacing of one's children, the right to privacy, the right to information, and the right to equality and nondiscrimination. Not only is guaranteeing access to contraception an integral part of these rights, but it is also a means to securing their fulfilment.

Moreover, guaranteeing access to available, acceptable, and good quality contraceptive information and services free from coercion, discrimination, and violence is critical for achieving gender equality and ensuring that women can participate as full members of society. The importance of contraceptives is highlighted by the fact that a range of them is included in the World Health Organization (WHO) Model Lists of Essential Medicines. UN bodies (such as the Committee on Economic, Social and Cultural Rights) have indicated that provision of the drugs on this list is a core minimum obligation of states in realizing the right to health. Importantly, the obligation to provide contraceptives is classified as "immediate"—often also called the "minimum core obligations"—meaning that this obligation is not dependent on the socioeconomic context and thus should be fulfilled immediately.

A rights-based approach (RBA) to the provision of reproductive health care and contraceptive information and services can guarantee the fulfilment of states' obligation and the concomitant realization of women's fundamental human rights. And it's really crucial to understand that access to contraception is mostly about preventing unwanted pregnancies in the developed North, but in the Global South it really is a life-and-death matter. While the life-quality enhancement and human rights fulfilment related to the provision of appropriate family planning is difficult to overestimate, the tragic and potentially life-threatening consequences of restricting access to contraceptives may result in devastating social, economic, and public health consequences. For example, of the approximately 80 million women who annually experience unintended pregnancies, 45 million have abortions. As a result, approximately 68,000 women die from botched back-alley abortions each year and complications from unsafe procedures are a leading cause of maternal morbidity. Research has shown that satisfying the current unmet need for contraceptives could prevent roughly 150,000 maternal deaths and 25 million induced abortions worldwide annually.

It really is a no-brainer—preventing unwanted pregnancies allows women and families to lead a measurably better life and prevents deaths (of mothers as well as children). Access to contraceptives is a human right and it's important to keep that in mind, when we veer towards perceiving it as a privilege of the richer or better educated.

> *"The nation's leading pediatrics group said . . . that intrauterine devices and implants should be the first option for teen girls who are having sex."*

Teens Should Have Access to IUDs

Kimberly Leonard

In the following viewpoint, Kimberly Leonard reports on health experts' suggestion that teenagers should have easy access to intrauterine devices (IUDs), which are inserted into the uterus and left there to prevent pregnancy. Leonard highlights experts' opinions on the effectiveness of these birth control devices and their potential benefits for teens. She also points out that in the current environment, it is difficult for teen girls to obtain these beneficial birth control devices. Leonard, a University of Richmond graduate, is a health care reporter for U.S. News & World Report.

As you read, consider the following questions:

1. According to Leonard, how effective are IUDs?

2. According to Leonard, why are IUDs difficult to obtain for anyone?

3. According to Leonard, why are IUDs particularly difficult for teenage girls to obtain?

The nation's leading pediatrics group said this week [in
September 2014] that intrauterine devices [IUDs] and
implants should be the first option for teen girls who are having sex—a notable update to its previous birth control guidelines that specified only condom use. But although the devices
are effective, safe and endorsed by most medical groups, teens
trying to get them can face hurdles, from their cost to the
stigma attached to adolescent sexual activity.

"We as a society need to work to reduce those barriers and
help teens to prevent pregnancy more effectively," says Dr. Eve
Espey, former chairwoman of the American College of Obstetricians and Gynecologists' Committee on Health Care for
Underserved Women.

The academy's statement encourages pediatricians to include abstinence as part of contraceptive counseling, advising
teens to delay sex until they are ready. But the group also says
pediatricians should remember that data suggest many teens
who plan on being abstinent do not remain so, and that doctors should "provide access to comprehensive sexual health information."

Birth Control and Obamacare

The advice comes as a heated debate over contraception continues to unfold in the political and legal arenas. The [Patient
Protection and] Affordable Care Act, or Obamacare, mandates
that insurance companies cover contraception services, even
for teens. But policy makers, women's health groups, businesses and religious rights groups are continuing to revisit this
particular detail.

The Supreme Court ruled this summer that private companies can deny birth control coverage for religious objections, and a Republican state representative in Missouri attempted earlier this year to sue the federal government because

he and his wife said they did not want to violate their Catholic beliefs by paying for their daughters to have access to birth control.

Meanwhile, some local health agencies are pressing forward with providing increased access to birth control. Colorado this summer released figures that showed the state's birthrate plummeted to 40 percent, a change officials attributed to IUD handouts from 2009 to 2013. The $23 million project—called the Colorado Family Planning Initiative—was funded by an anonymous donor.

Health officials in Colorado also pointed to other statistics of success, including a reduction in the teen abortion rate by 35 percent and a $42.5 million reduction in health costs associated with teen births.

How IUDs Work

Though lawsuits during the 1970s have continued to stigmatize the use of IUDs—a type of [birth control device] which back then had a design flaw that may have caused infections and sterilization—the medical community says IUDs now are safe. Doctors insert the device into a woman's womb, and it can prevent pregnancy for three to 10 years. IUDs are T-shaped and contain hormones or copper, with a plastic string tied to the end that hangs through the cervix into the vagina.

Implants, which are plastic rods the size of a match, are placed under the skin of a woman's upper arm and can prevent pregnancy for three years.

Both methods are reversible but do not prevent against sexually transmitted infections. Their side effects are similar to oral contraceptives and can include irregular bleeding, breast tenderness, acne, nausea or headaches.

The Centers for Disease Control and Prevention [CDC] started tracking IUD and implant use among teens last year, finding that less than 2 percent use such a method. According to the CDC, the unplanned pregnancy rate for women who use an IUD is between 0.2 percent and 0.8 percent, and the rate of unplanned pregnancies for implants is 0.05 percent. Women who take oral contraceptives have a 9 percent risk of unintended pregnancy, while condoms carry an unplanned pregnancy rate of between 18 and 21 percent.

The American Academy of Pediatrics, however, still recommends condom use among teens in order to protect from sexually transmitted infections.

"[IUDs and implants do not] require women to remember to do something to prevent pregnancy every day—like the pill—or just before intercourse, or once a month, or even every three months, like other methods," says Dr. Vanessa Cullins, vice president of external medical affairs at Planned Parenthood Federation of America. "Once an IUD or implant is inserted, you can pretty much just forget about it."

IUD Roadblocks

Despite their effectiveness, barriers to IUD and implant use are plentiful. Espey says many pediatricians are not trained on how to place IUDs or implants, and studies also suggest pediatricians are not talking to minors about sex and pregnancy prevention options—even though the American Academy of Pediatrics reports that half of all high school students have had intercourse.

A study published in the *Journal of Pediatrics* this year found that just 20 percent of 1,000 teens in Pennsylvania and New Jersey had their sexual histories documented by their pediatrician during a routine checkup, and a 2012 study by the CDC found that 30 percent of doctors and other providers doubted the safety of IUDs for women who have never given birth.

For some, the implantation procedure also can be expensive. An IUD typically costs between $500 and $1,000, which covers the exam, insertion and follow-up visit. Over the long

Why Teens Need Birth Control

It's hard to think of a segment of the American population that could benefit more from long-acting contraceptives than the teenager. Effectively using birth control can be difficult no matter how old you are, but preventing pregnancy presents singular challenges for adolescents. There's the mortification of fitting a condom over an unripe banana in front of your peers in health class. There's not necessarily wanting your parents to know that you're having sex, and so not using their insurance to pay for birth control. Then there's maintaining consistency in *anything*—from condom use to SAT prep—a feat that is hard when you're overwhelmed by homework, hormones, and the demands of being almost old enough to be in charge of yourself.

Adele Oliveira,
"What Happens When You Give Teenage Girls Free IUDs?,"
Jezebel, March 24, 2015.

term, the cost is less expensive than other forms of birth control, but can be difficult up front. Implants run between $400 to $800.

The costs are a huge barrier for women, Espey says, adding that companies are charging more for the devices than they cost to manufacture.

"There's truth to that for every pharmaceutical product," says Adam Sonfield, a policy expert on insurance and the Affordable Care Act with the Guttmacher Institute, a nonprofit that advocates for reproductive health. The companies will say the costs of the devices go beyond manufacturing, and that they need to recoup their investments in areas like research and development, testing and marketing, he says.

Under Obamacare, most health insurance plans will cover the implantation procedures, says Michelle Larkin, a spokeswoman for Teva Pharmaceutical Industries, which manufactures IUDs. Some plans do not yet offer contraception coverage because they are grandfathered plans, meaning they are gradually changing the benefits they provide and will eventually offer the services to comply with Obamacare. Family planning clinics that are funded by the federal government also provide IUDs to minors.

Teens and IUDs

For teens, however, there often can be another layer of difficulty: They may feel they can't approach their parents about paying for the procedure, and their parents could see it on an insurance bill if they obtain it on their own. The method would not appear on a bill if paid for out of pocket, but few teens have the resources to do so.

Confidentiality laws for minors on Medicaid vary by state, meaning some minors could access contraceptive services without their parents' consent. But there are teens who face abuse or being thrown out of the house if it's known that they're sexually active, Sonfield says.

"Minors do need the right and ability to consent to sensitive health services like contraception, mental health care, substance abuse services and other issues they may be reluctant to talk to adults about," he says, adding that he finds most teens are able to discuss these issues with their parents.

Though exemptions for birth control coverage are provided to religious groups, many states have taken a stance that care needs to be available for teens when they need it, Sonfield says. The District of Columbia and 26 states allow people between 12 and 18 to consent to contraceptive services without their parents' permission, according to the Guttmacher Institute, while 20 states allow some minors—including those that are married, face a health risk or are parents—to consent.

The four remaining states do not have a specific law related to contraception services and consent.

> *"The American Academy of Pediatrics issued a new recommendation that physicians promote the progestin implant and the intrauterine device (IUD) for teen girls. As the father of six girls—including three teenagers—I find this new recommendation particularly disturbing."*

Teens Should Not Have Access to IUDs

Eric Scheidler

In the following viewpoint, Eric Scheidler argues against granting teenagers unrestricted access to intrauterine devices (IUDs), which are inserted into the uterus and left there to prevent pregnancy. He outlines several key reasons why IUDs are a bad choice for teenagers and encourages parents to embrace an abstinence-only approach to teaching their children about sex and sexual activity. Scheidler is an ardent pro-life activist and the communications director for the Pro-Life Action League.

As you read, consider the following questions:

1. According to Scheidler, how would making IUDs available to teens undermine the relationship between those teens and their parents?

2. According to Scheidler, how would making IUDs available to teens be setting a double standard on adolescent health?

3. According to Scheidler, how would providing teens with IUDs increase the incidence of abortion?

Yesterday [in September 2014] the American Academy of Pediatrics [AAP] issued a new recommendation that physicians promote the progestin implant and the intrauterine device (IUD) for teen girls. As the father of six girls—including three teenagers—I find this new recommendation particularly disturbing.

It's not just that I bristle at the thought of a doctor asking my daughters a battery of questions about sex, as the AAP recommends. It's that I know how upset they would be to hear sexual acts they've never given a thought to presented as perfectly normal, or even expected of them.

Why the AAP Recommendation Is Wrong

Some might accuse me of being naïve, but they don't know my girls. And that points to the first of four reasons the new AAP recommendations are wrongheaded.

1. They undermine the role of parents.

In the new AAP recommendation, doctors are strongly discouraged from involving parents in their daughters' contraceptive use, even in states where the law doesn't require such "confidentiality." Though a nod is given to abstinence, moral questions about sex have no place in this private discussion between doctors and young girls, according to the AAP.

The message to teen girls is that—contrary to what their parents, church community and even their own well-formed consciences may have told them—there is no moral choice involved in whether or not to have sex.

Sadly, it should come as no surprise that this AAP recommendation would undermine the role of parents. One of the authors, Gina Sucato, is a member of the pro-abortion group Physicians for Reproductive Health, and testified against a parental notification bill in Washington State. Such measures are overwhelmingly supported by the public.

2. They weaken teens' choice not to have sex.

Though you wouldn't know it looking at our entertainment and news media, teen sex has actually been on the decline for over two decades—13% since 1991. How much more might it have declined in the absence of the constant barrage of messages teens are exposed to, telling them that everybody's doing it and you're kind of weird if you're not?

Now add to that your own family doctor, with the door closed to your mom and dad, suggesting that you might want to have progestin implanted in your arm or an IUD inserted so you can have sex without worrying about pregnancy for years on end.

The message is clear: You can't be counted on to make good choices. First, you can't be counted on to take a pill every day (which is why the AAP is pushing implants and IUDs). Nor can you be counted on to decide not to have sex, despite all the reasons it's not a good idea.

Yet, somehow, you can be counted on to use a condom to prevent STDs [sexually transmitted diseases]. Sort of.

The AAP's attitude towards condoms is particularly puzzling. In defending the new preference for implants and IUDs, they point out how inadequate condoms are for preventing pregnancy—both because teens often don't want to use them, and even when used they have at least an 18% failure rate. But then, they insist that condoms are absolutely necessary, each and every time a girl has sex, lest she get an STD.

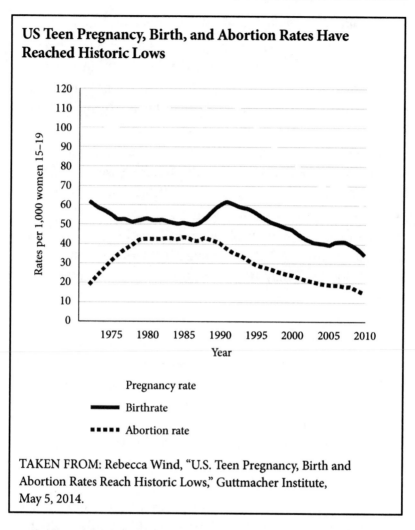

US Teen Pregnancy, Birth, and Abortion Rates Have Reached Historic Lows

Pregnancy rate

━━━ Birthrate

▪▪▪▪▪ Abortion rate

TAKEN FROM: Rebecca Wind, "U.S. Teen Pregnancy, Birth and Abortion Rates Reach Historic Lows," Guttmacher Institute, May 5, 2014.

Back to the implants and IUDs, as one of my adult sons asked, what kind of impact will it have on a girl should it become known around school that she's using one of these long-term methods of birth control?

Finally, the headlines accompanying the new AAP recommendation are discouraging both to teens who are abstaining from sex and the parents, pastors and educators who want to encourage that choice. What, instead, might be the impact of headlines announcing the AAP's support for abstinence as the best choice for teens?

3. *They set a double standard on adolescent health.*

Even as parents and coaches are trying to discourage the boys on the football team from using steroids to improve athletic performance, the AAP is encouraging the girls on the cheerleading squad—or the volleyball team—to have steroid-releasing devices implanted in their bodies.

That's what the artificial hormones in these devices are: steroids. Why the double standard? Shouldn't we be protecting both our sons and daughters from artificial steroids, and the health risks associated with them?

One of the long-term birth control methods being recommended by the AAP doesn't release hormones: the copper IUD. However, it may be more problematic for my final objection.

4. *They ignore the abortifacient potential of the IUD.*

It was because the IUD has the potential to cause an early abortion that Hobby Lobby objected to providing the devices without copay in their high-profile lawsuit against the HHS [US Department of Health and Human Services] mandate. The U.S. Supreme Court ruled that the owners of such closely held corporations cannot be forced to violate their moral objection to abortion by being required by the government to include abortion-inducing drugs in their health plans.

But the AAP has no problem promoting the IUD to teen girls without disclosing its abortifacient potential, which is completely ignored in the new birth control recommendations to doctors—despite the fact that teen girls might choose differently if they knew the IUD could cause an early abortion.

We already know that one of the coauthors of the new recommendation is a radical abortion advocate. Not only did she speak out against parental notification, she signed an amicus brief with the Supreme Court in opposition to the federal ban on partial birth abortion—again, a position at odds with the moral judgment of most Americans.

But however strongly Gina Sucato supports abortion, shouldn't she and her colleagues at the AAP seek to respect the pro-life views of their patients? Don't they have an ethical responsibility to disclose the fact that an IUD may prevent a newly conceived human being at its embryonic stage of life from implanting in its mother's uterus?

In these new recommendations on birth control for teen girls, the AAP has adopted a cavalier attitude not only toward girls' best interests and parents' relationships with their daughters but also to the value of life itself.

I encourage parents to contact the AAP to respectfully voice your objections to the new recommendation and call on them to emphasize abstinence as the only good choice for our daughters.

> "One of the most exciting recent news stories was the ... announcement that a male birth control shot could hit the market as early as 2017."

Male Birth Control Is a Necessity

Zoe Zorka

In the following viewpoint, Zoe Zorka argues in support of the development of a male version of a birth control shot. She contends that male contraception would have numerous social, economic, and other benefits for men and women alike. Zorka is a Utah-based writer who writes for the Elite Daily online news platform and has published her own fictional novel, Turn Our Eyes Away.

As you read, consider the following questions:

1. According to Zorka, why would male contraception be a victory for feminism?

2. According to Zorka, in 2013 how many people were receiving food stamps?

3. According to Zorka, what is one of the worst responsibilities for individuals?

One of the most exciting recent news stories was the Parsemus Foundation's announcement that a male birth control shot could hit the market as early as 2017.

As someone who has always promoted fairness and equality, this is incredible news that could offer positive repercussions for males and females alike.

It could ultimately help our society in the long term. Here are five reasons why male birth control might be the best advent we've seen in years.

1. It balances the scales of equality.

For far too long, a man's future has been in the hands of the woman with whom he shares a bed. There are so many stories of men who were surprised to become fathers after being unaware of their partners' birth control regimens.

While the most obvious answer might be to use a condom, men are still often subject to manipulation.

2. It supports true feminist ideals.

Back in the 1940s and 1950s, women had little to no option for birth control, and in some states, her husband had to approve before she could get it.

There was little recourse for marital rape, and if a man wanted a baby . . . well, he could probably force it to happen.

Today, women wouldn't stand for such things. So, why do we find it acceptable for women to make men unwilling fathers? As a rational feminist, I believe that only two willing parents should be able to conceive a child. (Side note: This fully includes gay and lesbian partners who choose to bring a child into the world through whichever means they choose.)

3. It could help our economy.

According to the Centers for Disease Control and Prevention [CDC], in 2012, nearly 41 percent of births were to out-of-wedlock mothers.

The Benefits of Male Birth Control

I don't want my only birth control options to be a condom, vasectomy, or trusting her. Those aren't enough choices. Furthermore, birth control is something men don't think about right up until they have sex. In addition to reducing accidental pregnancy, the male pill would increase male responsibility, awareness, and understanding of birth control *in general*. As a result, our society's understanding of sex, reproduction, and relationships would change *again* and for the better. Human enhancement is all about overcoming biology, and the male pill would be one heck of a step forward.

Kyle Munkittrick,
"Why I Want a Male Birth Control Pill,"
Discover, *March 28, 2011.*

In 1999, Isabel Sawhill of the Brookings Institution provided congressional testimony that showed a strong correlation between the increase in single-parent families (mostly due to unwed motherhood in the past few decades) and "virtually all of the increase in child poverty since 1970."

While some single mothers do stay with their partners, 60 percent of partners split within four years past the baby's birth, thus putting the family under significant financial strain.

Even in low-income households, two parents raising children together are economically far better off than most single mothers.

In 2013, the federal government's food stamp program served 46 million people. Two-thirds of the families were single-parent (usually mother) homes. Fewer single-mother births would most likely correlate to a decrease in the number of Americans living in and born into poverty.

4. It could save the children . . . literally.

Other studies show that children born to single mothers are not just more likely to end up in poverty, but also at higher risk for developmental delays, social problems, depression and suicide. Also, they are less likely to attend college than their peers who were raised with two parents (even if the parents were divorced).

Far too often, when a woman chooses to keep a baby a man does not want, she is also sentencing the child to a life of poverty, depression and shame.

Our planet is at a drastic risk of becoming overpopulated, so if we reduce the number of births in general, we can focus more resources on helping a more narrow group of tomorrow's children.

5. It's the morally right thing to do.

Basically, if a man were to drug his wife, get her pregnant and force her to bear a child, he would probably go to jail for a very long time.

However, right now, if a woman has a child with an unwilling male participant, she can go to court and get child support, while still getting money from the federal and state government, as well as a host of other social services.

Why? Child support (unlike alimony) isn't considered income under tax law. So, if a man pays a woman $4,000 a month in child support ($48,000 per year, tax free), and she does not work, it still appears that she has zero income, and she can file for SNAP [Supplemental Nutrition Assistance Program, which provides food purchasing assistance], Section 8 housing [rental assistance] and other benefits.

Now, I'm certainly not placing all blame on women. Of course, there are deadbeat dads who are to blame, as well. I'm also not suggesting that everyone needs to get married, either.

However, being an unwilling parent is one of the worst responsibilities for said unwilling individuals to take on—both for them as people and for their children.

We have empowered women to fight this fate, so now it's time that we extend the same right to men.

> "It should be up to both partners to pro-
> tect themselves from unwanted preg-
> nancy, but at the end of the day, the
> woman is the one who needs to protect
> her own body."

Male Birth Control May Disempower Women

Kaitlin Reilly

In the following viewpoint, Kaitlin Reilly argues against the idea of a male birth control pill on the grounds that it would not be beneficial to women. She contends that a male birth control pill would leave single women with less control over their reproductive activities and whether or not they get pregnant. Reilly is a contributing writer for the Bustle website.

As you read, consider the following questions:

1. According to Reilly, when would a male birth control be advantageous?

2. According to Reilly, how would a male birth control pill change the sexual balance of power between men and women?

3. According to Reilly, why would a male birth control pill be particularly problematic for single women?

Jezebel recently published an article about how it sucks that women are still waiting around for a great male equivalent of a birth control pill. According to the article, one of the main reasons why we have yet to see a male BCP [birth control pill] out there is because of the side effects associated with current trials of the hormonal pills used to stop the sperm from swimming, so to speak, don't outweigh the possible risks that come from a man having unprotected sex. Basically, because a dude doesn't actually have to deal with an unwanted pregnancy, the side effects are making these pills pretty hard to market—even though there's plenty of support for the pill from both men and women.

While I understand the arguments for wanting to get a male hormonal birth control on the market, I don't know if it's going to be the solution everyone thinks it is. Why? Well, for one thing, I just don't think that a male version of birth control is going to have many benefits for single women.

Problems with a Male Birth Control Pill

Let's imagine a scenario where we live in a world where men have access to a safe, effective hormonal birth control with limited side effects. A man in a monogamous relationship may choose to take a hormonal birth control pill in order to prevent pregnancy with his partner. In this case, it's not all that different from a woman choosing the female birth control pill (or other female birth control option). If a woman struggles with finding the right birth control option and isn't a fan of barrier methods, then the male taking the BCP is a convenient solution for the couple. I am completely for this, and I would love for women to feel like they had more options in terms of pregnancy prevention.

What I'm more concerned about is the implications that a male birth control pill will have for single men and women. I refuse to trust anyone else with protecting my interests—my interests being *not getting pregnant*—and think that it's important for women to feel empowered in terms of knowing how they are protecting their own bodies. Personally, I would feel far more comfortable knowing that I took control of my own body and was responsible with my birth control method than relying on someone else with far less at stake to protect me. Call me cynical, but what proof would a woman have that the person she's having sex with is really on the male birth control pill? Not a whole lot other than his word, and that absolutely terrifies me. (Oh, and did I mention that we're all living in a world where STIs [sexually transmitted infections] aren't a thing, either? Because that's one thing that no pill can protect you against getting from a partner.)

I am all for the idea of a male birth control pill. I really am, but I'm not buying that it's the answer to unwanted pregnancy. I think it will take some pressure off women to go on hormonal birth control, which is important for women in committed relationships who want to protect themselves without the often icky side effects. (Personally, I adore my hormonal birth control, but I know a ton of people who consider it a necessary evil.) For single women, I think that it's important to get as much visibility as possible when it comes to protecting against pregnancy. Unfortunately, you'll never be able to tell if a guy is really on birth control, just as a guy should never assume a woman is on hormonal birth control. I would much rather see women take an active role in their own safety with insistence on condoms or other types of barrier contraceptives for pregnancy prevention.

It should be up to both partners to protect themselves from unwanted pregnancy, but at the end of the day, the woman is the one who needs to protect her own body.

Periodical and Internet Sources Bibliography

The following articles have been selected to supplement the diverse views presented in this chapter.

Logan Albright	"Is Contraception a Human Right?," Ludwig Von Mises Institute, October 10, 2013.
Manny Alvarez	"Dr. Manny: Why I Would Never Recommend an IUD for My Teenage Daughter," Fox News, September 29, 2014.
Charlotte Andersen	"Women Weigh In on the Problem with Male Birth Control," SheKnows, September 17, 2014.
Center for Reproductive Rights	"Access to Contraception Worldwide Is Key to Women's Human Rights," December 10, 2013.
Arielle Duhaime-Ross	"The Best Contraceptives for Teens Are IUDs and Implants, CDC Says," The Verge, April 7, 2015.
Elaine Lissner	"Men Deserve Birth Control Options, Too," *New York Times*, January 2, 2014.
Amanda Marcotte	"Parents, Get Your Teenage Daughters the IUD," *Slate*, September 30, 2014.
Hillary Mast	"IUDs for Teens? Endangering, Not Empowering, Docs Say," Catholic News Agency, October 12, 2014.
Arikia Millikan	"The Perfect Birth Control for Men Is Here. Why Can't We Use It?," *Motherboard*, April 1, 2015.
Veronica Thomas	"Word to Pediatricians: IUDs and Implants Top Choices for Teen Birth Control," WBUR, September 29, 2014.

OPPOSING
VIEWPOINTS®
SERIES

CHAPTER 2

How Does the Affordable Care Act Affect Birth Control?

Chapter Preface

In the ongoing national debate over birth control, few topics are as controversial or heated as the birth control mandate in the Patient Protection and Affordable Care Act, commonly known as the Affordable Care Act (ACA) or Obamacare. In an effort to finally reform the country's ailing health care system, President Barack Obama sought in his first term in office to introduce a new national health care program. After much political struggle and compromise, his plan eventually came to fruition in the form of the ACA. The ACA made it easier for people to gain access to quality health care and affordable health insurance. In part, this was accomplished through the inclusion of an employer mandate that required businesses with more than fifty full-time employees to provide those employees with a health insurance plan. While this was ostensibly an important step forward for American health care, the employer mandate included some provisions that quickly proved to be problematic.

Among other things, the employer mandate required many employers to provide their employees with coverage for various forms of birth control. Although most employers affected by the mandate had no objection to this requirement, some did. A number of religiously affiliated employers balked at the idea of being forced to provide coverage for certain types of contraception that they believed cause abortions. They felt that the ACA—because it required them to pay for contraceptives to which they were morally opposed on religious grounds—violated their constitutional right to freedom of religion. Eventually, this dispute led Hobby Lobby, an Oklahoma-based retail craft store chain owned by an evangelical Christian family, to file suit against the federal government. By June 2014, the case made it all the way to the US Supreme Court.

The Hobby Lobby case was, at once, a microcosm of the furious birth control mandate controversy and the seminal dispute that would ultimately determine the law's future. While Hobby Lobby and its supporters railed against the perceived threat to their religious freedom, the ACA's supporters argued that bowing to such pressure would be an affront to women's rights and an opening for religious coercion. More to the point, the ACA's supporters believed that exempting religiously affiliated employers from the birth control mandate would prevent women in need from having access to quality reproductive health care.

Ultimately, the Supreme Court sided with Hobby Lobby, allowing it and other closely held for-profit businesses with religious affiliation to claim the same exemption already extended to religious nonprofit organizations. That exemption allowed Hobby Lobby and other companies to provide coverage for contraception at no cost to them through separate insurance policies.

The ACA birth control mandate and the Hobby Lobby decision are likely to continue to play a major role in the future of American health care and women's access to affordable contraception. The following chapter examines how the ACA affects birth control for women in the United States.

> "We are failing to meet an extremely
> basic health need for millions of women
> and their families across our country.
> It's time to stop allowing the issues to
> get co-opted and start demanding our
> lives, our families, and our futures are
> recognized."

Employers Should Provide Coverage for Birth Control

Alissa Light

In the following viewpoint, Alissa Light criticizes the US Supreme Court's 2014 decision in Burwell v. Hobby Lobby Stores *and argues that it is imperative that a way to adequately meet women's reproductive health needs be found. In her criticism, Light dismisses Hobby Lobby's objection to the Patient Protection and Affordable Care Act's birth control mandate and defends the status of contraception as an important part of women's health care. Light is the executive director of the Family Tree Clinic, a family planning facility in St. Paul, Minnesota.*

As you read, consider the following questions:

1. According to Light, why is it particularly troubling that Hobby Lobby scoffed at providing coverage for the specific types of contraception that it did?

2. According to Light, what percentage of pregnancies in the United States are unintended?

3. According to Light, contraception is the most ubiquitous health care need for how many women a year?

Today [June 20, 2014] the Supreme Court ruled on the Affordable Care Act's (ACA) contraceptive coverage requirement in the case of *Burwell v. Hobby Lobby Stores.*

Spoiler alert: They ruled in favor of Hobby Lobby, in a 5-to-4 decision.

Hobby Lobby is a for-profit arts and crafts store chain that employs more than 13,000 individuals. It sued the government for infringement of its right to exercise religious freedom under the Religious Freedom Restoration Act. The company brought suit in order to limit the contraceptive coverage made available on the insurance plan it provides employees. Hobby Lobby did this even though a majority of Americans believe employers shouldn't be able to opt out of the contraceptive coverage mandate.

Under the ACA, the government set forth a set of health insurance coverage requirements for basic health care services—which includes a full range of FDA [Food and Drug Administration–]approved birth control methods. Access to contraception is one of the most basic sets of health care, in fact. Several national polls report that nearly *99% of all women* use some kind of birth control method, at some point in their lives.

Objections to Certain Contraceptives

Now, to be clear, Hobby Lobby was not objecting to providing insurance that would cover contraceptives in general—only a

Hobby Lobby and Women's Health

"The Court, I fear, has ventured into a minefield," Justice Ruth Bader Ginsburg wrote in a strong dissent from a 5–4 ruling, issued by the Supreme Court on Monday [June 30, 2014], in favor of Hobby Lobby, a for-profit corporation that runs a chain of craft stores and wanted an exemption from part of the Affordable Care Act because it was, its owners said, against their religion. In particular, the owners were unwilling to pay for coverage for certain contraceptives. Justice Samuel Alito, writing for the majority, said that he had "no trouble" concluding that this sort of insurance coverage "substantially burdened" the owners of Hobby Lobby—burdened them morally, if not financially. . . .

Alito sees all the substance in how put-upon the owners of corporations feel. In oral arguments, [Justice Anthony] Kennedy openly worried that companies would somehow be mixed up with abortion, and one suspects that his sense that abortion is a distinctly volatile, morally charged subject was part of why he acquiesced here, and why he seems to believe, against all reason, that this decision is narrow. Women's health is treated as something troublesome—less like other kinds of health care, which a company should be asked to pay for, than as a burden for those who have to contemplate it. That is bad enough. But the Hobby Lobby decision is even worse.

Amy Davidson,
"A Very Bad Ruling on Hobby Lobby,"
New Yorker, June 30, 2014.

choice few that its leaders believe fall outside of their definition of contraception. This point—of cherry-picking contraceptive options approved by the FDA—is disturbing, and terrible public health policy. The methods they object to happen to include extremely effective, long-term methods that have grown in popularity and accessibility over the past few years. Long-acting reversible contraceptives—intrauterine devices [IUDs] and implants—are effective anywhere from 3–12 years and are changing the face of reproductive health and family planning because they remove from the equation two of the most common birth control barriers—user error and cost. When covered by health insurance, these methods are likely to be one of the single most effective and economical points of health care for women of reproductive age.

And we as a nation are in desperate need of effective, long-lasting contraception. Why? The United States has one of the *highest* rates of unintended pregnancy among developed nations. Just how high is it? Nearly 50 percent. Half of all pregnancies in the United States are unintended. That's one out of every two pregnancies. And if you are a low-income woman, your rate of unintended pregnancy is five times higher than that of a woman at the upper end of the income spectrum.

When we compare our teen birthrate to others, we fare even worse. According to the United Nations demographic yearbook, our teen birthrate is higher than the rate in the United Kingdom, Ireland, Israel, Canada, Germany, France, Norway, Italy, Sweden, Denmark, the Netherlands and Switzerland. We are tied with Romania, and Bulgaria leads by a hair. What is clear to me in today's ruling is that our nation continues its collective failure to support women, particularly low-income women, to have true access to the tools to plan their families and ultimately their futures.

Part of Basic Care

The ACA has made incredible leaps in addressing some of the major barriers by making health insurance more accessible and ensuring that coverage meets basic public health standards—like covering FDA-approved birth control. In fact, bi-partisan efforts at the federal and state levels have worked for decades to make contraception more accessible. For roughly *37 million women a year* the most ubiquitous health care need is contraception. And I bet a good proportion of the 13,000 individuals employed by Hobby Lobby fit this profile. Ensuring birth control is included as part of a basic set of covered health benefits makes social, economic and pragmatic sense.

Contraception is a basic health care need that will span just about 30 years of a person's life (the average span of a woman's potential reproductive years). It might be hard to imagine a 27-year-old woman working three low-wage jobs to come up with $25 extra dollars a month to buy a pack of birth control pills. It may be hard to relate to the 35-year-old mother of three whose husband's employer is cherry-picking health coverage, which means she can't get her birth control injection this month. It might be hard to think about having to choose between groceries or birth control today. Except that it isn't. Thirty-seven million people a year need access to contraception. Half of us have been or will be pregnant as a result of such difficult choices, and the other half of us know someone who has had to make that choice.

We are failing to meet an extremely basic health need for millions of women and their families across our country. It's time to stop allowing the issues to get co-opted and start demanding our lives, our families, and our futures are recognized.

"As long as that bad ingredient—the principle that government may coerce people to buy things for others—is baked into the cake, it will be rotten no matter how it's nicely decorated."

Employers Should Not Have to Provide Coverage for Birth Control

Sheldon Richman

In the following viewpoint, Sheldon Richman argues against the Patient Protection and Affordable Care Act's birth control mandate. He contends that the mandate's primary intent—to force employers to cover the cost of birth control for their employees—is fundamentally flawed. Richman roundly criticizes the mandate and suggests that it simply oversteps the boundaries of what truly constitutes a right. Formerly the editor of the Freeman, *Richman is a professional writer and the author of* Separating School & State: How to Liberate America's Families.

As you read, consider the following questions:

1. According to Richman, what do supporters of the Affordable Care Act consistently get wrong about why some companies are opposed to the birth control mandate?

2. According to Richman, why is it a fallacy to assume that women will suffer if their employers do not provide them with birth control?

3. According to Richman, the controversy at hand is not about contraception but rather is about what?

When you bake a bad ingredient into a cake, no matter how nicely you decorate it, the cake will still be bad.

That's the lesson to take from the controversy over Obamacare [referring to the Patient Protection and Affordable Care Act], Catholicism, and contraception. To recap, under Obamacare all employers will be required to arrange for "health insurance" for their employees. Coverage must include various disease-preventive health services and women's contraception *at no charge.* No premium sharing, no co-pays, no deductibles—nothing.

The Department of Health and Human Services [HHS], which has ominous rule-making power under Obamacare, exempted Catholic churches (as employers) from this rule because Catholicism teaches that contraception is sinful. However, HHS did not exempt Catholic institutions whose mission (the government says) extends beyond religion, namely, colleges, hospitals, and charities. Those institutions would have to pay (nominally at least) for their women employees' birth control products and services.

That seemingly arbitrary distinction set off a political firestorm intense enough to force the [Barack] Obama administration back to the drawing board. Under President Obama's so-called "accommodation," all Catholic institutions would be exempt from paying for contraception after all, *but* their insurance companies would have to provide the coverage at no cost.

Top Catholic officials are still unhappy, though other prominent Catholics are satisfied. The matter isn't settled yet. (Aside: Is there a significant difference between a Catholic institution's being forced to pay for employees' birth control and its being forced to arrange the match between its employees and the insurance company that will pay for it?)

In announcing his "accommodation," Obama said that religious liberty has been squared with a "core principle": "a law that requires free preventive care will not discriminate against women." We need not "choose between individual liberty and basic fairness for all Americans." Since men's contraception is not mandated for free coverage, Obama's remark about discrimination is puzzling.

Competing Liberty Interests?

Washington Post columnist E.J. Dionne, a Catholic and an enthusiast for Obamacare, put it this way: "There were legitimate liberty interests on both sides of this debate." He is satisfied that both "liberty interests" have been served.

What exactly are the two liberty interests? One is clear: An institution wishes not to be compelled to facilitate what it regards as morally abhorrent. (The validity of that moral judgment is irrelevant.) But what's the other one? One infers from the discussion that it's women's liberty to use contraception. (A third liberty interest—an insurer's right not to be forced to give away services—is strangely overlooked.)

How exactly was the liberty to use contraception jeopardized by the Catholic exemption? In no way would a woman's *freedom* in this respect be infringed simply because her employer was free to choose *not to pay* for her contraceptive products and services. . . .

Yet advocates of Obamacare insist on conflating these issues. They repeatedly portray opposition to *forced financing* of contraception as opposition to contraception itself. (Alas, some conservatives have encouraged this conflation.) Must the difference really be spelled out?

This sort of argument is nothing new, of course. In *The Law* (1850), Frédéric Bastiat noted that advocates of government-run schools accused those who opposed them of being against education itself.

Prohibitive Expense

When pressed, proponents of "free" employer-provided contraception claim (as though this were responsive) that many women can't afford birth control and that insurance companies would save money by giving it away. (Why haven't the insurers thought of that?)

Taking these in reverse order, the second argument begs the question. Insurance companies allegedly would save money because they wouldn't have to pay for medical services associated with having children. That assumes that if the insurer were not providing free contraception, women would have to do without. *But that is precisely what is in dispute.* Why assume that?

As for the claim about the allegedly prohibitive expense, one may properly ask how *that* could justify forcing others to pay. It's amusing to watch advocates of free contraception cite as evidence for their position polls showing that women overwhelmingly support no-cost contraception. Since when have people not wanted free stuff? Women have managed to obtain birth control up until now (we're repeatedly told that nearly all women, including Catholics, have used it), and low-income women can resort to Planned Parenthood [Federation of America] if necessary, which already gets taxpayer money (which is not to say it should).

When a "Right" Is Not a Right

What we have in this debate is a clash not between two liberty interests, but rather between two rights-claims—one negative (genuine), the other positive (counterfeit). All that is required for the exercise of a negative right (to self-ownership and, redundantly, liberty and one's legitimately acquired belongings) is other people's noninterference. ("When we say that one has the right to do certain things we mean this and only this, that it would be immoral for another, alone or in combination, to stop him from doing this by the use of physical force or the threat thereof," writes James A. Sadowsky, S.J.) But the fulfillment of positive rights requires that other people act affirmatively *even if they don't want to*—say, by providing products or paying the bills. If one person's freedom depends on the infringement of someone else's freedom, the first claim is illegitimate. To hold otherwise is to reject the principle of equality.

Women have the right to contraception (and any other product) in the sense that they have a right to spend their money on it or to try to *persuade* someone else to do so. There can be no right to *force* (or have the government force) others to pay. (Aside #2: It's curious to see feminists asking the male-dominated state for "free" birth control.)

This controversy is not about contraception. It's about freedom versus compulsion.

As long as that bad ingredient—the principle that government may coerce people to buy things for others—is baked into the cake, it will be rotten no matter how it's nicely decorated.

> *"There is no delegation to Congress in the U.S. Constitution of authority to institute a program of national health insurance, let alone dictate to employers and underwriters what private employee health plans must cover."*

Is Religious Freedom the Issue with the Contraceptive Mandate?

Jack Kenny

In the following viewpoint, Jack Kenny argues that the Patient Protection and Affordable Care Act, also known as Obamacare, birth control mandate—and even the act itself—is unconstitutional. He contends that the government is overstepping its constitutional boundaries with the Affordable Care Act and infringing on Americans' right to religious freedom and on corporations' right to protection from undue government intervention. Kenny is a contributing writer for the New American, *a periodical focused on the US Constitution and constitutional issues in politics.*

As you read, consider the following questions:

1. According to Kenny, how is the birth control mandate a violation of the First Amendment?

2. According to Kenny, why is the idea of national health care inherently flawed?

3. According to Kenny, what is wrong with the birth control mandate's interpretation of personal liberty?

The First Amendment of the Constitution of the United States is a mighty defense against tyranny, and the first of the five freedoms named therein (Quick: Can you name them all?) is the free exercise of religion, which accompanies the prohibition on an establishment of religion by Congress. Since Article I of the Constitution places all legislative powers in a Congress of the United States, the ban was understood to prohibit an establishment of religion by the federal government period, before a substantial power of lawmaking was taken over by the justices of the Supreme Court.

Still, it is at least debatable that the optimum strategy for opposing the contraceptive mandate under Obamacare is to claim it violates the religious freedom of the employer. That certainly is the strategy of the U.S. Conference of Catholic Bishops, which, after decades of lobbying for Caesar to please give us a national health care program, discovered that the one we finally got includes (surprise!) a requirement that all employer-based health insurance programs include coverage of contraceptive products and services, including abortion-inducing drugs, with no deductible or co-pay. Other employers, including Hobby Lobby and Conestoga Wood Specialties Corp., claim that while their businesses are for-profit corporations, the mandate also violates the religious freedom of conscience of the owners, who are evangelical Christians and Mennonites, respectively. The companies' objections were argued Tuesday at the U.S. Supreme Court.

Indeed, the program, as it now stands, offends the First Amendment in myriad ways. To begin with, it gives the government the power to decide which organizations qualify as, for the purposes of receiving an exemption from the mandate, religious institutions. The Amish apparently qualify, given their voluntary isolation from secular society and people of other faiths. But Catholic or other religious-affiliated schools and hospitals do not qualify, since they both hire and serve people of other faiths and thus their internal policy decisions do not all flow from their adherence to the doctrines of their respective churches. Thus, the government policy is said to protect employees of other faiths or no faith from being limited in their health care decisions by a restrictive policy based on someone else's religion. But this sets a dangerous precedent in that it empowers the government to determine what is or is not a religious institution, a practice that might reasonably be considered a government establishment of an overarching religious authority in violation of the First Amendment's establishment clause.

The root problem is in the collectivist notion of national health care in the first place. The premise is that given a universal right to health, to the extent that the patient's constitution and the resources of modern medicine allow, it is up to the national government to provide health care insurance for all, especially for those who can least afford it. Hospitals are generally in favor of such a requirement because, though most are officially charitable organizations, their need to provide uncompensated care is reduced, if not eliminated, by a government program that requires people to pay for health insurance and subsidizes those who can't afford a policy. Some small businesses might welcome the program since it provides the option of getting out of health insurance altogether and letting employees get their coverage from one of the government's health insurance exchanges. It also provides an inducement for small business to reduce their number of full-

The Birth Control Mandate Is Unconstitutional

The American public is witnessing a fascinating, even historic, event: the [Barack] Obama administration's attempt to suppress basic expressions of religious faith.

The Department of Health and Human Services (HHS)'s recent rulemaking mandating that church-sponsored and affiliated enterprises that provide health insurance must also provide contraception coverage audaciously defies the religious liberty predicate that this nation is founded upon. It furthermore threatens our long-held belief that all Americans may worship and serve God free from governmental interference.

It also is a direct violation of the First Amendment.

Horace Cooper,
"The Birth Control Mandate Is Unconstitutional,"
National Center for Public Policy Research, February 2012.

time employees to get out from under the Obamacare requirement that businesses with over 50 full-time employees offer health insurance. Unfortunately, that leads to fewer full-time jobs and more unemployed or part-time workers who need full-time jobs. Not a good development for the health and wealth of the nation.

People who have no job would likely prefer to have a job with no health insurance than have no job and no health insurance. More to the point, most would be pleased to have both a job and health insurance, even if that insurance did not cover the things provided for in the contraceptive mandate. Some of the arguments offered in defense of the mandate run from the weak to the pathetic. Suppose, goes one hypothetical, a Jehovah's Witness or Christian Science employer objected to health insurance that covers blood transfusions. But the contraceptives do not involve a do-or-die emergency situation. One might think that, absent a government program, diaphragms and birth control pills would be rarer than hens' teeth. Opinion polls have shown for a long time that many, perhaps most, women of childbearing age have been availing themselves of such amenities for years, even decades. Most women of a certain age and intelligence can readily find them. What the Obamacare mandate represents is the iron fist of compulsion attempting to enforce contraception as a societal good and making all who believe otherwise to bend the knee to Baal.

The courts, to be sure, have been more open to arguments about religious freedom than legal briefs demonstrating that, high court decisions to the contrary notwithstanding, the authority of Congress to control (the actual term is "regulate") interstate commerce is not really the Eighth Wonder of the World, broader than the Grand Canyon and Gobi Desert combined. There is no delegation to Congress in the U.S. Constitution of authority to institute a program of national health insurance, let alone dictate to employers and underwriters what private employee health plans must cover.

Some will argue that the Supreme Court upheld the constitutionality of the Obamacare program (the Patient Protection and Affordable Care Act) in its June 2012 decision. But the justices upheld the individual mandate, imposing fines for uncovered individuals who do not purchase health care plans, by declaring it to be a tax, despite language in the legislation saying it is not, rather than an exercise of the congressional power to regulate interstate commerce.

As for personal liberty, the argument of Planned Parenthood and the Obama administration is that employees should not be restricted in their reproductive choices by the religious scruples of their employers. But the freedom to practice contraception does not, to a reasonable person, imply a responsibility of others to provide it for them. Were that the case, the Congress might require employers to honor the First Amendment's freedom of the press guarantee by providing their employees with journalism courses free of charge.

Interestingly, neither contraception nor the right of access to it are mentioned anywhere in the Constitution. They became constitutional issues by a Supreme Court ruling (*Griswold v. Connecticut*) that the freedom to contracept is covered by a fundamental right to privacy. But if it's wholly a matter of privacy, why must there be a public program, supported by taxpayers' dollars, to provide for it?

Employers are legally persons, too, at least until the Supreme Court rules otherwise. They also have rights, including the right to religious freedom. More to the point, they have the right to be left alone from unauthorized, unconstitutional government mandates. That's why we have a Constitution in the first place.

> "To focus on the religious liberties of
> employers while overlooking those of
> their employees . . . is . . . to set back
> the cause of liberty and justice for all."

The Affordable Care
Act Birth Control Mandate
Is Constitutional

Jonathan D. Sarna

*In the following viewpoint, Jonathan D. Sarna argues that the
Patient Protection and Affordable Care Act's birth control mandate does not constitute a violation of the right to religious freedom. He instead suggests that denying people health care coverage for procedures or products that are contrary to certain
religious beliefs is actually a form of religious coercion. In short,
Sarna contends that the birth control mandate is, indeed, constitutional. Sarna is the Joseph H. and Belle R. Braun Professor of
American Jewish History at Brandeis University and chief histo-
rian of the National Museum of American Jewish History.*

As you read, consider the following questions:

1. According to Sarna, how is Catholic employers' refusal
   to cover the cost of birth control for their employees an
   example of religious coercion?

2. How does Sarna respond to Rabbi Meir Soloveichik's assumption about those who employ people of different faiths?

3. What solution does Sarna suggest for addressing the problem of birth control coverage?

Invoking George Washington's famous letter to the Jews of Newport, R.I., Rabbi Meir Soloveichik of New York's Congregation Kehilath Jeshurun, one of the foremost Orthodox rabbis of his generation, told a congressional committee on February 16 [2012] that requiring health insurance plans to cover contraception threatened "the liberties of conscience" of fellow Americans and "redefined by bureaucratic fiat" the definition of religion itself. He found it appalling that any religious organization—Catholic or not—should be "obligated to provide employees with an insurance policy that facilitates acts violating the organization's religious tenets."

In many ways, it is heartwarming to see an Orthodox rabbi standing up for the religious liberties of his Catholic cousins. Many of us felt ashamed when so many rabbis failed to do this in 2010, when the religious liberty of Muslim Americans was challenged during the controversy over building a mosque near Ground Zero. As a minority group that has fought hard for religious equality, and one that rightly takes pride in having received from Washington himself the assurance that religious liberty is an "inherent natural right" that cannot be abridged, we should all feel obliged to testify whenever religious liberties are challenged.

Religious Freedom vs. Religious Coercion

Yet for all that one may sympathize with Catholic institutions coerced into promoting contraceptive services that they consider sinful, Soloveichik's congressional testimony greatly oversimplifies the religious liberty conundrum confronted by those who oversee national health insurance. The guarantee of religious liberty, after all, applies not only to religious organizations, but also to individual citizens. However much Catholic institutions may invoke religious liberty when they deny those they employ access to contraception, it is critical to remember that from the perspective of those employees, the denial reeks of religious coercion.

The analogy to "forcing kosher delis to sell ham," put forward by Bishop William Lori, exemplifies the way the problem is misunderstood. In America (unlike in Israel), people have the right to choose whether they want to sell ham and whether they want to consume it; neither option is proscribed. We all might agree that kosher delis should not be coerced into selling ham, but hopefully we would also all agree that a deli's employees and customers should not be penalized for choosing to consume it.

Similarly, a kosher deli routinely gives its employees a day off on Yom Kippur, a fast day. But the deli would not be within its rights if it provided that benefit to only those employees who fast on Yom Kippur; that would be coercive. Denying insurance claims for contraceptive services represents the same kind of coercion. In First Amendment terms, the contraception issue represents a classic tension between the "no establishment" and "free exercise" clauses of the First Amendment. What Soloveichik understandably sees as a limit upon Catholic institutions' free exercise of their religion, employees of Catholic institutions see, no less understandably, as an attempt to "establish" Catholic doctrine coercively. The Supreme Court generally privileges the "no establishment" clause over the "free exercise" clause in such cases. It certainly does not ignore "no establishment" claims, as Soloveichik does.

Soloveichik, in his testimony, takes particular exception to a distinction that the government has drawn between religious employers who hire only members of their own faith and are permitted to conduct their affairs according to church tenets

Do You Agree or Disagree with the Following Statements?

Employers should have the right to choose what forms of contraceptives their health plans provide, based on their religious beliefs.

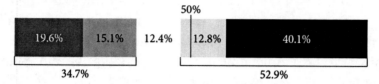

50%

| 19.6% | 15.1% | 12.4% | 12.8% | 40.1% |

34.7%   52.9%

Employers should not have the right to prevent certain forms of preventative health care including contraceptives from being provided in their health plans based on their religious beliefs.

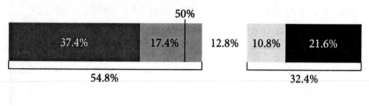

50%

| 37.4% | 17.4% | 12.8% | 10.8% | 21.6% |

54.8%   32.4%

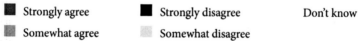

■ Strongly agree   ■ Strongly disagree   Don't know

▨ Somewhat agree   ▨ Somewhat disagree

Should for-profit businesses be allowed to apply for federal law exemptions based on the employer's religious beliefs?

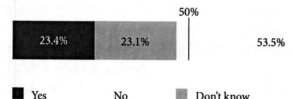

50%

| 23.4% | 23.1% | 53.5% |

■ Yes   No   ▨ Don't know

Note: 10,693 adults interviewed online, April 28 to June 27. Credibility interval: ± 1.1 percentage points. Source: Reuters/Ipsos.

TAKEN FROM: Tara Kulp-Ressler, "Most Americans Want Hobby Lobby to Lose Its Supreme Court Case," *ThinkProgress*, June 30, 2014.

and religious employers who hire members of multiple faiths and are obligated by the government to accommodate them.

"The administration implicitly assumes," he charges, "that those who employ or help others of a different religion are no longer acting in a religious capacity and as such are not entitled to the protection of the First Amendment."

In fact, the government makes no such assumption at all. Instead, it reasonably assumes that employers and employees both have First Amendment rights, including the "no establishment" right not to be religiously coerced. Precisely for this reason, chaplains in the military who certainly act in a religious capacity are prohibited from evangelizing those of other faiths, even when their religion otherwise requires them to do so. Where members of different religions dwell together (even when they do so under religious auspices), securing them all the right to the "free exercise" of their faith is much more conducive to social harmony than allowing employers to impose their faith requirements on their employees coercively.

Finding a Solution

Is there any way of satisfying both the religious strictures of the church and the religious predilections of its employees? If, as in most Western countries, the burden of acquiring health care were placed upon individuals rather than employers being required to provide it, then everyone could choose for himself or herself whether to have a plan with contraceptive benefits. Those with other strong beliefs about health care (such as Christian Scientists) could similarly select plans that accord with their faith. Nobody would be coerced, and everybody could purchase the plan that he or she wants.

Meanwhile, one hopes that Congress will ignore the testimony of Soloveichik. To focus on the religious liberties of employers while overlooking those of their employees, and to focus on only the free exercise clause of the First Amendment while ignoring the dangers of coercive religious establishments, is to pervert what Washington meant when he spoke of "liberty of conscience" and to set back the cause of liberty and justice for all.

"Most importantly . . . the burden on the women involved 'would be precisely zero.' They will get the same free contraception that the challenged rule would have provided. In short: good for women, good for religious liberty."

The Hobby Lobby Decision Was a Victory for Women's Rights

Andrew Koppelman

In the following viewpoint, Andrew Koppelman argues that the US Supreme Court's decision in Burwell v. Hobby Lobby Stores *was, contrary to popular belief, a positive outcome for women's rights. He explains that in ruling in favor of Hobby Lobby and, more importantly, granting religiously affiliated for-profit companies the same exemption to the Patient Protection and Affordable Care Act's birth control mandate already provided for religious nonprofit companies, the Supreme Court crafted an ideal solution that respected both the religious rights of Hobby Lobby and the personal rights of the women it employs. Koppelman is an author whose works include* The Tough Luck Constitution and the Assault on Health Care Reform *and* Defending American Religious Neutrality.

As you read, consider the following questions:

1. According to the viewpoint, why was the government's interest in guaranteeing the availability of free birth control not compelling?

2. According to Koppelman, why would it have been a disaster if Hobby Lobby had been granted a full exemption from covering the cost of birth control for its employees?

3. According to Koppelman, why was the Supreme Court's final decision a win for religious freedom and women's rights?

Monday's Supreme Court decision in *Burwell v. Hobby Lobby* could have been a disaster for women's health and equality and, in the long run, for religious freedom. The court cleverly devised a solution that avoided that disaster and decently accommodates the interests that had collided. The decision was a small victory for women's equality—a core issue that many lower courts casually ignored.

The Affordable Care Act requires many employers to provide comprehensive insurance coverage, including contraception. Contraception can be expensive: an intrauterine device (IUD), one of the most reliable methods, can cost over $1000. Hobby Lobby, a chain of craft stores, and several other companies objected to this requirement. The owners tried to run their businesses on religious principles, and they regarded some contraception as a form of abortion.

The federal Religious Freedom Restoration Act of 1993 (RFRA) prohibits the government from burdening a person's exercise of religion unless that burden is the least restrictive means of furthering a compelling government interest. Hobby Lobby claimed, and many lower federal courts agreed, that the government's interest in guaranteeing cost-free access to contraceptives was not compelling, because there are plenty of ex-

The Hobby Lobby Balancing Act

Anthony Kennedy, in an opinion concurring with the majority in [*Burwell v. Hobby Lobby Stores*], . . . seems to find the best way of balancing . . . two sides:

> Among the reasons the United States is so open, so tolerant, and so free is that no person may be restricted or demeaned by government in exercising his or her religion. Yet neither may that same exercise unduly restrict other persons, such as employees, in protecting their own interests, interests the law deems compelling.

> In other words, nobody gets to be "right" in this case. No one's religious beliefs can trample someone else's health needs, and even if the government can't force closely held private companies to pay for contraceptives, these companies can't stop their employees from being on birth control. *Hobby Lobby* is a balancing act, not a bludgeon—and certainly not an attack on women's rights.

Emma Green, "The Supreme Court Isn't Waging a War on Women in Hobby Lobby," *Atlantic, June 30, 2014.*

ceptions to the mandate. Obamacare exempts employers with fewer than 50 employees, which leaves 20 to 40 million employees uncovered. It does not apply to grandfathered plans, which cover millions more. An interest with so many exceptions, they reasoned, could not be a compelling one. Some of those courts also said that religious liberty could not be outweighed by a vague, generalized interest in "the promotion of public health." One court was clueless enough to conceptualize the problem as one of determining the harm to the *government* if the exemption is granted.

The reasoning here is strained. The exemptions in question are mostly temporary. It is hard for a plan to keep its grandfathered status. More importantly, it shouldn't be hard to decide whether the interests in question are compelling. When contraception is expensive, fewer women use it. Unintended pregnancies are awful for the women involved. They're also bad for the children: Women who don't know they are pregnant are more likely to drink or smoke and less likely to get prenatal care. The contraception mandate improves the health of pregnant women and newborns, reduces the disparity in health costs between men and women, and, most importantly, allows women to determine the course of their own lives. Involuntary impregnation is one of the nastiest things that one human being can do to another. If promoting women's health, bodily integrity, liberty and equality is not a compelling state interest, then what would be?

Some courts also concluded that, if Congress really wanted to provide contraception, it could pay for it itself. So they deemed the law to flunk the least-restrictive-means requirement. This rested on pure fantasy. Everyone knows that the Republican Congress will never vote such a subsidy.

In those now superseded decisions, the upshot was that women who worked for those employers—a *lot* of women; Hobby Lobby has over 13,000 full-time employees—got no contraception coverage.

That made Hobby Lobby and other religious employers happy. But in the long run it would have been a disaster for religious liberty. That idea has always rested on the claim that one person's religion doesn't hurt anyone else. In Thomas Jefferson's classic formulation: "[I]t does me no injury for my neighbour to say there are twenty gods, or no god. It neither picks my pocket nor breaks my leg."

Had Hobby Lobby won on the grounds it claimed, however, religious liberty would suddenly mean the right to impose your religion on other people who don't share your views. Such a pronouncement by the court would certainly have strengthened the already growing secularist movement to eliminate any special legal protection for religious freedom.

Instead, the court assumed, without deciding, that the government's interest was compelling. Doubtless some members of the five-judge majority disagreed with that, but Justice Anthony Kennedy's separate concurrence signaled pretty clearly that he thought so, and Justice Ruth Bader Ginsburg's dissent, for four justices, was even clearer. That's a majority of the court. So what could have been a disaster for women's equality suddenly became a victory.

Having found a compelling interest, the court moved on to least-restrictive burden. Here it ignored the bogus subsidy option, and noted instead that the Obama administration had crafted a clever solution for religious nonprofits. Those companies' insurers were required to provide contraception in separate policies, for free—something the insurers were happy to do, because even expensive contraception is cheaper than childbirth.

The court's decision essentially required that the same accommodation be extended to religious for-profit employers. That will create some administrative headaches, which is why the administration resisted. But the alternative was imposing a heavy burden on the owners of Hobby Lobby, who clearly take their religious scruples very seriously.

Most importantly, as Justice Samuel Alito noted in his majority opinion, the burden on the women involved "would be precisely zero." They will get the same free contraception that the challenged rule would have provided. In short: good for women, good for religious liberty. It's a clever resolution that none of the parties had asked for, but that is better than anything on the menu that the court had before it.

> *"Employers who object to birth control on religious grounds may now refuse to comply with federal rules requiring them to include contraceptive care in their health plans. The rights of the employer now trump the rights of the employee."*

The Hobby Lobby Decision Was Misguided

Ian Millhiser

In the following viewpoint, Ian Millhiser argues that the US Supreme Court's decision in Burwell v. Hobby Lobby Stores *was a misguided attempt at ensuring religious freedom that may have dire civil rights consequences. He suggests that the ruling leaves religious organizations with the ability to unjustly force their beliefs on others. This, he adds, may well be a threat to the civil rights of people whose lifestyles do not conform to religious standards. Millhiser is a senior fellow at the Center for American Progress Action Fund and the justice editor for the* ThinkProgress *blog.*

As you read, consider the following questions:

1. According to Millhiser, what makes Justice Samuel Alito's decision in *Hobby Lobby* a bait and switch?

2. According to Millhiser, how will religious organizations benefit from *Hobby Lobby?*

3. According to Millhiser, the biggest loser in *Hobby Lobby* may be whom?

For many years, the Supreme Court struck a careful balance between protecting religious liberty and maintaining the rule of law in a pluralistic society. Religious people enjoy a robust right to practice their own faith and to act according to the dictates of their own conscience, but they could not wield religious liberty claims as a sword to cut away the legal rights of others. This was especially true in the business context. As the Supreme Court held in *United States v. Lee*, "[w]hen followers of a particular sect enter into commercial activity as a matter of choice, the limits they accept on their own conduct as a matter of conscience and faith are not to be superimposed on the statutory schemes which are binding on others in that activity."

With Monday's [June 30, 2014] decision in *Burwell v. Hobby Lobby*, however, this careful balance has been upended. Employers who object to birth control on religious grounds may now refuse to comply with federal rules requiring them to include contraceptive care in their health plans. The rights of the employer now trump the rights of the employee.

To achieve this outcome, Justice Samuel Alito's opinion on behalf of a bare majority of the court engages in a kind of legalistic bait and switch. It takes a law Congress enacted to serve one limited purpose, and expands that law to suit Hobby Lobby's much more expansive purpose.

Legal Precedent

In its 1963 decision in *Sherbert v. Verner*, the court announced that laws that impose an "incidental burden on the free exercise of [a person of faith's] religion" may only be applied to them if the law is "justified by a 'compelling state interest in the regulation of a subject within the State's constitutional power to regulate.'" As anyone who has studied constitutional law will immediately recognize, this "compelling state interest" framework is the language judges use when they wish to invoke a test known as "strict scrutiny"—the highest test that exists under American constitutional law. Typically, laws that are subjected to strict scrutiny fare very badly. Strict scrutiny is the constitutional standard used to evaluate laws that discriminate on the basis of race, for example, and it only permits laws to be enforced when they further a compelling government interest and when they use the least restrictive means of doing so.

It soon became clear, however, that when the court considered religious liberty claims it was actually engaged in something much less rigorous than strict scrutiny. As Professor Adam Winkler documented, courts uphold less than one-third of all laws they subject to strict scrutiny—yet they rejected 59 percent of the claims brought by plaintiffs claiming religious liberty. A different study reached even starker results—determining that nearly 88 percent of religious liberty plaintiffs lost under the standard announced in *Sherbert*.

The most likely explanation for this fact is that *Sherbert* and its progeny were careful to maintain the balance between religious liberty and third parties' rights. In *Sherbert* itself, the justices emphasized that they were siding with a plaintiff who claimed a religious liberty right not to work on Saturday because "the recognition of the appellant's right" did not "serve to abridge any other person's religious liberties." Less than a decade later, in a case called *Wisconsin v. Yoder*, the court once again emphasized that it was exempting an Amish family from a law making school attendance mandatory because it did not perceive any harms to third parties. "This case," the court explained, "is not one in which any harm to the physical or mental health of the child or to the public safety, peace, order, or welfare has been demonstrated or may be properly inferred."

Ten years after that, the court decided the *Lee* case, with its proclamation that a business owner's own religious views "are not to be superimposed on the statutory schemes which are binding on others" engaged in a similar business. Allowing an employer to ignore a law protecting its employees, the court explained "operates to impose the employer's religious faith on the employees."

In 1990, however, the court briefly narrowed the protections offered to people who object to laws on religious grounds in an opinion authored by Justice Antonin Scalia. This unpopular decision inspired the Religious Freedom Restoration Act (RFRA), which formed the basis of Hobby Lobby's legal claim. Yet, the purpose of RFRA was not to change the longstanding balance between religious liberty and the rights of third parties. Rather, it was to restore the many decades of religious liberty law that began with the *Sherbert* opinion. Indeed, RFRA explicitly states that its purpose is to "restore the compelling interest test as set forth in *Sherbert v. Verner* [] and *Wisconsin v. Yoder* []."

Alito's Opinion

Justice Alito's opinion, however, tosses this explicit statement of congressional purpose aside, although he offers little explanation for why he is justified in doing so. His best effort is a reference to a 2000 law that amended one of RFRA's definitions of an "exercise of religion" to take out an explicit reference to the First Amendment. According to Alito, the purpose of this amendment was "an obvious effort to effect a complete

"WHATEVER YOU WANT, THE ANSWER IS NO. EVERYTHING IS AGAINST OUR RELIGION!"

separation from First Amendment case law" as laid out by cases like *Sherbert* and *Yoder*. Yet, it is difficult to square this interpretation with the fact that the RFRA statute still provides that its purpose is to "restore the compelling interest test as set forth" in *Sherbert* and *Yoder*.

The upshot of Alito's opinion is that, for the first time in American history, people with religious objections to the law will be able to ignore many laws with impunity unless the government's decision to enforce the law overcomes a very high legal bar that few laws survive. The full implications of *Hobby Lobby*, however, may not be known for years. When cases like *Sherbert, Yoder* and *Lee* were still good law at the federal level, plaintiffs alleging religious liberty alleged that they could engage in race discrimination and discrimination against women, and they also claimed immunity to paying Social Security taxes and the minimum wage. Though the Supreme Court probably isn't ready to revisit these cases, religious business owners are likely to find many other regulations they can now object to on religious grounds. And all of these objections will come to court with vigorous tailwind.

Alito goes to great pains to deny that his opinion will open up a parade of litigation enabling employers to deny other forms of health care coverage to their employees. The government, Alito notes, "points to no evidence that insurance plans in existence prior to the enactment of ACA [Patient Protection and Affordable Care Act] excluded coverage for a wide variety of medical procedures and drugs, such as vaccinations and blood transfusions." Nor, Alito writes, has the government "provided evidence that any significant number of employers sought exemption, on religious grounds, from any of ACA's coverage requirements other than the contraceptive mandate." This may very well be true, but there is an easy explanation for why it is true. Before the Supreme Court's decision in *Hobby Lobby*, employers who object to blood transfusions or vaccinations had no reason to believe they would win in court. *Sherbert, Yoder* and *Lee* were the law.

Alito also emphasizes that there are other steps the government could take to ensure that Hobby Lobby's employees have access to birth control, such as by paying for it themselves or by extending an accommodation for religious nonprofits so that it also covers private employers. For this reason, the biggest loser in *Hobby Lobby* may very well be LGBT [lesbian, gay, bisexual, and transgender] Americans. The courts are already swelling with business owners claiming that their religion entitles them to discriminate against gay people. Monday's decision does not ensure their victory, but their chances look much better now than they did just 24 hours ago.

In an ominous passage, Alito denies that his opinion will allow employers to engage in a particular kind of discrimination—"The Government has a compelling interest in providing an equal opportunity to participate in the workforce without regard to race, and prohibitions on racial discrimination are precisely tailored to achieve that critical goal." Left unspoken in this passage is whether the justices agree that the government has a compelling interest in preventing other forms of discrimination, such as discrimination against women or gay people.

Hobby Lobby and the Future

In fairness, Justice Anthony Kennedy writes in a concurring opinion that he may be less sympathetic to religious liberty claims in "which it is more difficult and expensive to accommodate a governmental program to countless religious claims based on an alleged statutory right of free exercise." That may reflect his unease with a future case claiming that religious belief is a license to discriminate against LGBT employees. In any event, however, Monday's decision casts a cloud of uncertainty over an area of the law that was quite settled 24 hours ago. And it does so based on little more than a bait and switch.

Periodical and Internet Sources Bibliography

The following articles have been selected to supplement the diverse views presented in this chapter.

Binyamin Appelbaum	"What the Hobby Lobby Ruling Means for America," *New York Times Magazine*, July 22, 2014.
Julie Borowski	"Hobby Lobby Decision Isn't About Birth Control, It's About Bullying," RedState, July 1, 2014.
Horace Cooper	"The Birth Control Mandate Is Unconstitutional," *National Policy Analysis*, February 2012.
Frederick Mark Gedicks	"With Religious Liberty for All: A Defense of the Affordable Care Act's Contraception Coverage Mandate," American Constitution Society for Law and Policy, October 2012.
Robert Jeffress	"Hobby Lobby Ruling: Why Supreme Court Got It Right," Fox News, June 30, 2014.
Jack Jenkins	"Why the Hobby Lobby Decision Actually Hurts People of Faith," *ThinkProgress*, June 30, 2014.
Damon Linker	"Why Liberals Should Cheer the Hobby Lobby Decision," *The Week*, July 1, 2014.
Patricia Miller	"What Do Religious Women Think of the Contraceptive Mandate?," *Atlantic*, March 22, 2015.
Amy Ridenour	"Ridenour: Employers Shouldn't Need to Pay for Birth Control," *Newsday*, January 16, 2014.
Jeffrey Young	"The Accidental Reason Companies Like Hobby Lobby Control Our Health Care," *Huffington Post*, June 30, 2014.

OPPOSING
VIEWPOINTS®
SERIES

CHAPTER 3

What Concerns Does Birth Control Raise?

Chapter Preface

For a variety of reasons, birth control remains a very controversial topic in the United States. Questions about the potential side effects of different contraceptive methods and the overall safety of birth control, as well as whether birth control options such as the pill and the patch should be available for purchase over the counter, are just a few of the concerns that make birth control such a hot-button issue. Perhaps the most divisive issue of the birth control debate, however, is the relationship between contraception and abortion.

More often than not, people's opinions on abortion—another hotly debated topic—tend to color their opinions on birth control. As such, many religious conservatives who strongly oppose abortion also oppose birth control, at least to some extent. At a minimum, these individuals generally object to any forms of birth control that they view as abortifacient, or capable of causing an abortion. This type of opposition is usually focused on contraceptive methods such as the morning-after pill, which may result in a fertilized egg being passed out of the womb. In such instances, anti-contraception advocates argue that the use of birth control results in the termination of a pregnancy and is therefore morally impermissible.

On the opposite side of this argument are those who adhere to the scientific explanation that birth control is not actually abortifacient. In their view, contraception's abortifacient potential depends entirely on the specific definition of pregnancy. Whereas pro-life advocates typically believe that life begins at conception, the scientific and medical communities hold that pregnancy does not actually begin until the fertilized egg becomes implanted in the uterus. The latter definition of pregnancy is key to the birth control debate because useful post-fertilization contraceptives only prevent fertilized eggs from becoming implanted in the uterus. They do not have any effect on implanted eggs. Because of this, birth control supporters argue that contraception, by definition, cannot be seen as a form of abortion.

There continues to be disagreement over whether birth control is the functional equivalent of abortion. As a result, it seems as though the broader controversy surrounding birth control has little chance of receding in the foreseeable future.

The following chapter examines the debate concerning over-the-counter birth control options, the dangers to women's health posed by hormonal birth control, and the use of emergency contraception such as Plan B and ella.

> "Standing up for [over-the-counter] birth control pills would absolutely be a hard, long fight, but it would be one that demonstrates that the pro-choice community really means it when we say we trust women with their own health care decisions."

Birth Control Should Be Available Over the Counter

Amanda Marcotte

In the following viewpoint, Amanda Marcotte argues that birth control pills should be made available over the counter. She says that the long-held belief that keeping birth control pills available only by prescription encourages women to visit their doctors regularly should be disregarded. She believes that if birth control pills were available over the counter, they would be more accessible and less stigmatized in comparison with other forms of birth control. Marcotte is a contributing writer for various websites and blogs as well as the author of It's a Jungle Out There: The Feminist Survival Guide to Politically Inhospitable Environments *and* Get Opinionated: A Progressive's Guide to Finding Your Voice (and Taking a Little Action).

As you read, consider the following questions:

1. According to Marcotte, the birth control pill is used as bait for what?

2. According to Marcotte, what can Planned Parenthood do to make over-the-counter birth control pills a feasible reality?

3. According to Marcotte, why would it be a good idea to couple birth control pills with condoms?

In all the fussing over the sale of emergency contraception over-the-counter (OTC), it's easy to forget that there's another contraception drug out there that should be available OTC but isn't: the ordinary, everyday birth control pill. The American College of Obstetricians and Gynecologists (ACOG) thinks birth control pills should be sold OTC. Most other countries sell birth control pills OTC. And now, as *Think-Progress* reports, nearly two-thirds of American women say they want the pill sold OTC, and about 30 percent who aren't currently on the pill would consider going on it if this option was available.

So why can't we have this, when the public and the medical establishment both think it's a great idea? Part of it is no doubt the politics of it. As the furor over emergency contraception—which you only take in emergencies (and don't need if you're consistent with your birth control pills)—demonstrates, the idea of women being able to prevent pregnancy easily sets off all sorts of irrational reactions in this country. You should have to struggle for it to prove you deserve to be not-pregnant, because . . . mmmph that's why. The religious right already believes that contraception is too easy to get, which is why they've been attacking it with so much vigor lately. Trying to make birth control pills available OTC would set off a political firestorm that would make the emergency contraception wars look like mere skirmishes.

Birth Control as Bait

Still, for women's health, I believe that's a fight that pro-choicers would be happy to have (though maybe not the folks in the [Barack] Obama administration trying to maintain the ruse that they better understand medical risk than researchers and doctors). The problem here, however, is that there's still a widespread belief that birth control pills need to be prescription-only in order to make sure women go to their doctors. Unlike many of the other countries that have the pill available OTC, the United States doesn't have universal health care (yet, though in 2014, we may see this shift dramatically due to Obamacare), which means that doctors have a uniquely difficult time in this country encouraging women to go to the doctor regularly. The argument is that we need to use the pill as bait to make sure women are going to their doctor—or to a local Planned Parenthood—to get their checkups.

It's a tempting argument, but something that needs to be tossed out for a number of reasons. First and foremost, as pro-choicers we need to adhere closely to the principle of supporting a woman's right to the ultimate authority over her own health care. If birth control pills are safe enough to be sold OTC, then it's up to a woman to decide if she wants a doctor's supervision to take them, just as we allow individuals to make that determination with other drugs, like allergy medications or pain killers.

Second of all, the science doesn't support the claim that using the pills as bait supports women's health better than de-coupling the pill from regular exams. Increasingly, research supports the conclusion that American doctors overuse the pelvic exam and the Pap test. Forcing women to take a major health risk with unintended pregnancy in order to get them to submit to a bunch of medical tests they may not even need is not good medical practice, especially when you consider that pregnancy requires massive medical intervention whether a woman chooses abortion or to bring the pregnancy to term.

Over-the-Counter Birth Control Pills

In many parts of the world, a person can walk into a drugstore and ... buy a pack of birth control pills over the counter. Perhaps several packs.

Not so in America, where the Food and Drug Administration (FDA) has been considering making oral contraceptives available over the counter (OTC) for more than twenty years. . . .

A woman with good health insurance and easy access to care could very well see a doctor for pill recommendations. But an undocumented immigrant, a sexually active 19-year-old whose parents disapprove, a woman in an abusive marriage, a woman who forgot to pack her pills while on vacation ... they wouldn't have to. They could walk into a drugstore, consult with a pharmacist, or not, and walk out with a tool to prevent pregnancy.

Elizabeth Nolan Brown,
"Over-the-Counter Birth Control Pills? Not in America,"
Reason, March 26, 2014.

Most importantly, there's no reason to believe that women will stop getting regular medical care just because they can buy the pills OTC. Prescription pills will be available without a co-pay for insured women under the Department of Health and Human Services (HHS) regulations, which will be plenty of encouragement for women to keep in regular contact with their doctors without taking away their right to choose. In addition, making pills available OTC could be met with creative responses to use the pill-buying experience as an opportunity to encourage women to get checked up by a gynecologist, albeit by the more relaxed new standards instead of the old, overly invasive routine.

Making Birth Control Available
Over the Counter

Planned Parenthood could play a major role in all this. Planned Parenthood clinics could continue to offer pills with a deep discount by tweaking their already existing practices slightly, but when women come to pick up their prescription-free pills, the staff could use that time to highlight other important services they offer. Knowing that they don't actually have to come in for invasive tests every year could encourage a lot of women who are currently hesitant to come in. Perhaps some of those 30 percent of women who aren't on the pill but would consider it if they could get it OTC would be reached. They aren't being reached now, if they avoid family planning clinics completely out of an overblown fear of being subject to too many tests. College health centers could play a similar role, offering the pills OTC but also including information on getting inexpensive and noninvasive checkups.

Right now, birth control pills being prescription-only means that they're decoupled from condom use. You can go pick up pills at the pharmacy counter without even walking by the condoms in most drugstores, creating this sense that there are "pill users" and "condom users," and that they don't even share an aisle. But if pills were sold OTC next to condoms, as emergency contraception soon will be, that creates an association. They could even be advertised as things to be used in conjunction with each other. If you're with a partner in a non-monogamous or non-tested relationship, it would make it much easier to think of yourself as someone who uses condoms first and the pill as backup.

We should charge ahead on this unafraid. Standing up for OTC birth control pills would absolutely be a hard, long fight, but it would be one that demonstrates that the pro-choice community really means it when we say we trust women with their own health care decisions. Putting more time and resources toward this also means picking another fight with the right over contraception, and history shows that's a fight that tends to favor our side in public opinion.

"Here's the thing: [Over-the-counter] birth control probably wouldn't be as simple and carefree as you think."

Should Birth Control Be Over the Counter?

Casey Gueren

In the following viewpoint, Casey Gueren argues that we should perhaps think twice about making birth control available over the counter. Citing a number of potential concerns, Gueren shows that even though over-the-counter birth control would be convenient, it would pose some challenges that might well negate its worth. At the time the viewpoint was written, Gueren was a contributing writer for Women's Health *magazine. Currently, she is the senior health editor at BuzzFeed.*

As you read, consider the following questions:

1. According to Gueren, how might making birth control available over the counter prevent some women from being able to get it?

2. According to Gueren, why might women have fewer contraceptive options if birth control were sold over the counter?

3. According to Gueren, even if some types of birth control were sold over the counter, not all types would be. In her opinion, why would this be a problem?

Imagine picking up your birth control at the pharmacy or grocery store whenever you need it—without worrying about a prescription or taking off a few hours from work to make an appointment with your gyno. Sounds fantastic, right? It's a premise that reproductive rights groups have been considering for years, and it's recently been cast into the spotlight again with several Republican candidates supporting it.

But here's the thing: OTC birth control probably wouldn't be as simple and carefree as you think.

"Over-the-counter birth control is an important concept," says Vanessa Cullins, MD, vice president of external medical affairs at Planned Parenthood Federation of America. "It is another vehicle to increase access to contraception. It should not be the *only* vehicle, and most definitely—just as it's stated in the Affordable Care Act legislation—contraception should still be available without a co-pay."

See, the current Affordable Care Act birth control benefit allows women to receive any FDA-approved contraceptive method without a co-pay, as long as they have a prescription. What many politicians are supporting is a system where birth control comes out onto the store shelves to be more convenient, but it likely wouldn't be covered at no cost.

The OTC Debate

The reason some politicians are in favor of this is that it seems to be a compromise to the birth control mandate. If birth control was available over the counter, insurance companies wouldn't have to cover the full cost and employers wouldn't have to worry about covering it if they had an objection. As we saw with the Supreme Court decision in favor of Hobby Lobby, not everyone is in favor of covering all birth control methods without a co-pay, so putting it over the counter would be a way to shift the responsibility and the payment to each individual who wants protection.

There's no doubt that making birth control over the counter would be more convenient in certain situations—like when you accidentally run out of refills and need them ASAP or when you want to start the pill but don't have time to schedule a gyno appointment.

That said, it could also create a barrier for women who can't afford birth control if the cost goes up (Cullins says there's no way of knowing at this time how much OTC birth control might cost). Unfortunately, more than half of women ages 18–35 report struggling with the cost of birth control at some point, causing them to use it inconsistently, according to a survey by Planned Parenthood.

Then, of course, there's the matter of what methods would even be available over the counter. Obviously, anything that needs to be inserted, like the IUD or implant, would not be available on a drugstore shelf. The birth control pill, the ring, and the patch could potentially be sold over the counter, as long as they meet all of the FDA criteria, says Cullins (this includes making sure people can understand the label, that they can determine whether or not they're an appropriate candidate for that particular drug, that it cannot be addictive, etc.).

Plus, if birth control became available over the counter, the OTC options for women would be more limited than what's currently covered under the Affordable Care Act. "There are well over 40 formulations of birth control pills," says Cullins, and each of those usually has a branded version and at least one generic. "So not every formulation will go over the counter."

This also means you would still need a prescription for the IUD, which is over 99 percent effective and the method used most by physicians. Sure, OTC pills would be more conve-

The Cost of Over-the-Counter Pills

One of the biggest issues customers have with any drug that was formerly available by prescription moving to OTC [over the counter] is that it often increases the cost. Insurance companies subsidize medications that are prescription-only, and customers often have only a small co-pay so, depending on the drug, being able to purchase it directly means more out-of-pocket expense. This already has happened with many allergy, antacids, and other medications. The cost increase would be even bigger when it comes to the birth control pill, since one of the provisions of the [Patient Protection and] Affordable Care Act is that those with insurance should be getting no-co-pay birth control already, eliminating your monthly expense. Put the pill in stores, and that will likely send you back to paying a bill every 28 days.

Robin Marty, "10 Things Every Woman Should Know About Over-the-Counter Birth Control," Cosmopolitan, *October 9, 2014.*

nient, but with a failure rate of about nine percent with typical use, they're not the most foolproof method out there.

So while this plan sounds like a simple fix at first, it may mean paying more money for more limited and less effective birth control methods. It could even result in women going for the cheapest or most convenient option, when that might not be what's actually best for her individual needs.

"There are no magic bullets," says Cullins. "No one birth control method tends to serve one woman throughout her entire reproductive life. Women will try different methods to see what works best for them and under which circumstances." But if some methods become OTC while others are available with a prescription and a co-pay, it might mean even more confusion for women just trying to find the right contraception for them.

What the Future of OTC Birth Control Looks Like

Perhaps the biggest problem with this debate is that politicians really can't control what medications are available where. "Congress cannot make any type of medication go over the counter," says Cullins. "That is a decision made in this country by the FDA and it is accompanied by research that is conducted by pharmaceutical companies." But get this: "As of now, there is no pharmaceutical company that has expressed concrete interest in taking [their method over the counter]," says Cullins.

For now, it's highly unlikely that any forms of birth control will be available without a prescription in the near future. "I've been involved with groups that have been discussing this for the past 10 years," says Cullins. "Given that, it really is safe to say it's going to be several years. There are additional studies that need to be done."

That's certainly not for lack of support for increased access. In one recent poll, 70 percent of Americans said they were in favor of over-the-counter birth control. And previously, the American College of Obstetricians and Gynecologists (ACOG) stated that oral contraceptives are safe enough for OTC availability.

"The hope is that we would have coexistence of over-the-counter methods and pills and other contraceptive methods that are covered by insurance without a co-pay," says Cullins. "But we don't know what the future will bring considering how charged this issue is."

In the meantime, stay informed about your contraceptive options and the latest news by visiting our birth control center.

"*Advocates say that women need to be talking more openly about the drawbacks of the pill as a cure-all—so we can push doctors, researchers, and the pharmaceutical industry to give us better options. Because right now, they're pretty limited.*"

Birth Control Can Be Dangerous to Women's Health

Virginia Sole-Smith

In the following viewpoint, Virginia Sole-Smith argues that women should pay closer attention to the side effects of the birth control pill and recognize that sometimes the pill is not the best contraceptive option. Citing her own difficult experiences with the pill, Sole-Smith contends that women should be cautiously critical of the pill so that they might enjoy maximum benefits and minimal risk. Sole-Smith is a writer whose work has appeared in such publications as Elle, Harper's, New York Times Magazine, *and* Slate.

As you read, consider the following questions:

1. According to Sole-Smith, why are birth control pills, especially those like Yaz, potentially dangerous for women?

2. According to Sole-Smith, why is there so much confusion about the proscribed benefits of birth control pills and their alleged side effects?

3. According to Sole-Smith, why do some women consider it dangerous to be critical of the pill's risky side effects?

When my gynecologist said I needed to go on birth control pills at age 14, my feminist mother rejoiced. I'd been missing several days of school every month since my period had started two years earlier, bringing with it vomiting, mind-numbing cramps, and the kind of heavy bleeding that ruins white jeans and fragile middle-school egos.

"Thank God for the pill," my mom said. "Now you won't have to suffer like I did." She came of age pre-Advil and spent the first three days of her period cradling a hot-water bottle and throwing up everything she ate. My grandmother had even more dire stories about surviving as a teenage girl in World War II England (that would be before Advil or ultra-thin maxi pads). The menstrual cycles of the Sole women have always been violent and all-consuming, but at last, liberation was at hand.

So I kept my pack of Ortho-Cyclen tablets next to my toothbrush and faithfully popped one at the same time each night. My cramps and nausea eased within a few cycles. While other girls were getting caught off guard by irregular periods that seemed to show up right before a trip to the beach, I knew almost to the hour when mine would start and stop. I also neatly sidestepped the angst of teenage acne, and when I started having sex a few years later, I had my contraception covered. Taking the pill made me feel in control of my body and my choices. It was everything feminists had fought for, all wrapped up in a purple plastic packet.

I wasn't the only woman being prescribed the pill for so-called off-label reasons—meaning any reason other than pregnancy prevention. More than 80 percent of sexually active U.S. women will use the pill at some point during their lives, the CDC [Centers for Disease Control and Prevention] reports. And, according to a 2011 Guttmacher Institute report, an estimated 58 percent of women currently taking hormonal contraceptives say they're not doing so to prevent pregnancy, or at least not only for that. Thirty-one percent use it to control cramps, 28 percent to regulate their cycles, and 14 percent to treat acne. In fact, 14 percent of current pill users cite one of these purposes as their sole motivation.

The pill has become not just a cure-all for "female troubles" but also a stand-in for reproductive rights. When Rush Limbaugh and his conservative brethren were attacking women's access to the pill through Obamacare [referring to the Patient Protection and Affordable Care Act], we all understood it to be an attack on women's rights. And this made me feel like a bad feminist when—14 years after I popped my first one—I began to have doubts about whether the pill was the silver bullet I'd initially thought.

When the Pill Is a Problem

At 28, bedeviled by side effects such as sore breasts, loss of libido, and migraines, I took my doctor's suggestion that I stop taking the pill. I had an IUD [intrauterine device] inserted instead. "Your cycle has been suppressed almost since you started having one," my doctor noted. "Let's see how you do if your body gets back in the driver's seat."

As it turns out, my body is a crap driver. While my sex drive did bounce back, the intense cramping and bleeding returned too. I developed an ovarian cyst that ruptured, producing a stabbing sensation that made regular cramps feel like warm hugs. In 2012, a month after my thirty-first birthday, I had surgery to diagnose and remove endometriosis.

Endometriosis is a chronic condition in which excessive estrogen causes the uterine lining that is normally sloughed off during your period to build up and grow in places it shouldn't, forming painful cysts and lesions on other reproductive organs. In the most severe cases, this rogue tissue can bind organs together or spread beyond the pelvis altogether, to the lungs and eyes. It afflicts as much as 10 percent of women of reproductive age, and between 30 and 50 percent of them are infertile. And it's a slow burn—as I soon learned, the average time between onset to diagnosis is 11 years. "Well, I guess I got lucky because I got diagnosed so quickly," I said to my surgeon.

"Actually, I think you waited a lot longer," he replied. "Most women with endometriosis report heavy periods and intense cramping in their early teenage years—but we put them on the pill right away, so we never know they have the disease." Indeed, one recent study published in the journal *Fertility and Sterility* confirms that women with moderate to severe endometriosis are four times more likely to have been prescribed the pill before age 18 to treat menstrual pain. Even when endometriosis is suspected (it can be formally diagnosed only via surgery), the pill is the most commonly prescribed treatment; doctors typically consider surgery or more aggressive drugs (which put you into a false menopause) only for women who can't find a version of the pill that stops the pain.

The Pill—What It Does

Most versions of the pill work by releasing a steady dose of synthetic progestin and estrogen throughout the month. These formulations squelch the production of the body's own reproductive hormones, and without the signals from the naturally made hormones, the ovaries don't release eggs, thus preventing pregnancy. But in the process, the pill spurs dozens of other physical changes, which is why it's become the first, and often only, line of attack to treat a raft of female troubles— whether serious medical conditions like endometriosis and polycystic ovarian syndrome (both of which can cause infertility and other complications) or more mild complaints such as acne, mood swings, PMS [premenstrual syndrome], or bloating. "The pill has become the major nonsurgical tool of gynecology," says Jerilynn Prior, MD, professor of endocrinology and metabolism at the University of British Columbia and founder and scientific director of the university's Centre for Menstrual Cycle and Ovulation Research.

Whether that's a positive or a negative depends on your perspective. To Christiane Northrup, MD, author of *Women's Bodies, Women's Wisdom*, prescribing the pill for debilitating menstrual conditions, such as the endometriosis I suffered from, only masks the problem. "It's like a mechanic putting a piece of duct tape over the indicator light on your dashboard and claiming he's fixed your car," she says.

But to mask endometriosis is also to slow its course, and to believers in the pill, which includes most of the gynecological establishment, so-called menstrual regulation has been a huge boon for women's health and personal freedom. "I've been in practice for 24 years, and this is always something we've done," notes Jeanne Conry, MD, president of the American Congress of Obstetricians and Gynecologists (ACOG).

Yaz

Granted, she says, the situation became more complicated when the FDA [Food and Drug Administration] began in the mid-2000s to let pill manufacturers tout what for decades had been off-label uses. There was Duramed Pharmaceuticals' Seasonique, which would allow women to "repunctuate" their lives by having just four periods a year, because "when you're on a birth control pill, there's no medical need to have a period." Then came the blockbuster drug Yaz, from Bayer Health-

Care Pharmaceuticals. Marketed as "beyond birth control"—with ads featuring the catchy tunes "Goodbye to You" and "We're Not Gonna Take it"—Yaz promised to alleviate acne, weight gain, mood swings, and menstrual headaches, owing to its low dose of estrogen and new form of progestin. It quickly became the country's best-selling hormonal contraceptive, with annual sales of more than $1 billion. The problem was, while all hormonal contraceptives can cause blood clots—about two cases per 10,000 women, but higher for those over 35 or who smoke or suffer from aura migraines—the FDA began receiving reports in 2009 that seemed to link Yaz to a higher incidence of the potentially fatal condition.

As a result, the agency requested that Bayer launch a $20 million ad campaign to set the record straight, but decided not to pull Yaz from the market when research, funded by the company, concluded that it carried no higher risk for blood clots than competing birth control pills. (Other reports have since put the clot risk for those who take Yaz as high as 10 cases per 10,000.) And an ACOG committee opinion published last year [2012] essentially affirmed the FDA's opinion, stating that women who don't have particular risk factors for clots can stay on Yaz.

So for most gynecologists, it's business as usual for the pill, leavened with a dash of caution regarding Yaz. "I have taken most of my patients off Yaz because there are so many other options out there," says ACOG president Conry.

It's this strategy of switching pills—rather than rethinking the readiness with which they're prescribed—that drives critics like Northrup and Los Angeles journalist Holly Grigg-Spall crazy. At 30, Grigg-Spall told her ob-gyn, a woman, that she planned to quit Yasmin (which is similar to Yaz but has a higher estrogen level) because she feared it had something to do with her depression, migraines, and insulin resistance, among other things. Her doctor didn't quibble with her decision—in fact, she said, "I'm not surprised; the pill made me

feel depressed for years until I came off it"—and then immediately suggested an alternative brand. The author of last
month's *Sweetening the Pill: Or How We Got Hooked on Hormonal Birth Control*, Grigg-Spall took the newly prescribed
pill for six months, she says, but her depression didn't lift until she quit using hormonal contraceptives altogether.

The Pill's Confusing Side Effects

There is a decent amount of data to buttress anecdotal reports
like Grigg-Spall's, including a recent study out of Australia
that garnered headlines with its conclusion that women on
the pill were twice as likely to experience depression, anxiety,
mental numbness, and an inability to feel pleasure from normal activities (known as anhedonia). These kinds of side effects can be among the most frustrating because they're so
easily dismissed by doctors and even by the women experienc-
ing them. "I kept thinking, Oh I'm just stressed out," says
Grigg-Spall. "Then after a while, you start to think, Maybe this
is normal for me. It's hard to connect it to your birth control."

The confusing upshot is that some women take the pill
precisely because they say it stabilizes their moods, while others say it disrupts theirs. To add one more perplexing twist,
Gillian Einstein, PhD, a neuroscientist at the University of To-
ronto who studies the biochemical effects of hormones on the
brain and cognition, says that when her lab measured women's
hormone levels, they found *no* correlation between subjects'
menstrual cycles and mood in the first place. "And yet, we
have entire industries built around the idea that women are
moody and irrational before their periods," Einstein says, suggesting that the idea that menstruation messes with women's
heads may be driven more by a culture that makes it difficult
for them to express anger than by their biochemistry.

As for whether the pill itself influences women's emotional
equilibrium, Einstein says she isn't sure. "This is a big open
question. We do know that hormones are very complex and

Side Effects of the Pill

A comprehensive meta-analysis published in the *Mayo Clinic Proceedings* noted that 21 out of 23 studies found an increased risk of developing premenopausal breast cancer in women who had taken the pill prior to the birth of their first child. Other side effects that women have experienced include high blood pressure, blood clots, stroke, heart attack, depression, weight gain, and migraines.

Chris Kahlenborn, "What a Woman Should Know About Birth Control," One More Soul, December 17, 2009.

act on every single body system." Lab experiments have shown that estrogen affects single neurons in the brain, she says, but how that specifically pertains to mood or behavior is still a mystery.

Criticizing the Pill

It feels dangerous to complain about the pill when retro-minded legislators in every state and most branches of the federal government are determined to chip away at women's right to choose, and 49 percent of our nation's pregnancies are unplanned. After all, in June 2013 Wisconsin's state assembly passed a bill limiting women's access to contraception . . . , and the FDA tried to make the morning-after pill available only to women over age 15, despite a federal judge's ruling—and this was at the behest of the relatively liberal [Barack] Obama administration. "The pill and contraception in general have become so tied to our conversation about abortion that it's really difficult to talk about honestly," says Laura Eldridge, author of *In Our Control: The Complete Guide to Contraceptive Choices for Women.* "It feels like giving fodder to the other side. I understand those anxieties, but it's not in the service of women to avoid talking about these realities." Eldridge says she's been asked to speak to anti-choice organizations eager to scare girls away from contraception altogether. "Any criticism of birth control has been co-opted completely by people with a very anti-woman, anti-sex agenda," Grigg-Spall adds. "And that's partly the fault of the women's movement. We've let [the Right] take control of the conversation."

Instead, these advocates say that women need to be talking more openly about the drawbacks of the pill as a cure-all—so we can push doctors, researchers, and the pharmaceutical industry to give us better options. Because right now, they're pretty limited. On the contraception front, IUDs are gaining ground, but fewer and fewer doctors are prescribing basic yet effective methods like the diaphragm or condoms. The "fertility awareness method," once the sole province of religions that didn't allow other forms of contraception, has been newly embraced by holistic women's health experts such as Northrup, who says it can be at least 95 percent effective when used correctly. She says, however, this requires that "women interact consciously with their fertility, and the reality is that many women still don't have conscious dominion over their fertility. Or they're just too busy. There are times in many women's lives when it makes sense to put your pelvis on autopilot."

Finding a Solution

For other problems, the list of alternatives is even shorter. To treat endometriosis, polycystic ovarian syndrome, and hormonal infertility, Prior likes to use a naturally derived progesterone, called Prometrium, because it doesn't get metabolized into estrogen in the same way that synthetic progestins do. But so far her strategy hasn't caught on among her fellow physicians. Prior and Northrup both encourage women to explore how diet, exercise, stress, and other lifestyle factors impact their reproductive health.

But when I asked my surgeon about such approaches for my endometriosis, he shrugged and said, "We have no idea whether any of that makes a difference." A classic and infuriating surgeon's response, yes—but I'm here to say that when you're living in pain, you don't want to hear how maybe giving up refined sugar or doing more yoga will make things better in three months. You want a pill that makes you feel better. Now.

There's the rub. We still want the convenience, freedom, and empowerment that the pill delivered when it hit the market in 1960. And it does have some serious upsides: Few things beat the pill for pregnancy prevention, and it substantially reduces a woman's chances of getting very lethal cancers like endometrial and ovarian cancer (however, some studies have shown the pill may raise the risk of breast cancer while women are taking it and for up to 10 years after they stop).

None of the pill critics I interviewed wanted to limit a woman's access to the drug if she is happy with it. "The pill works very well for many, many women," Eldridge says. It's the rest of us, however, who could use a little more attention from mainstream medicine.

As for me, I'm still on hiatus from the pill, for an unexpectedly cheerful reason: Despite my endometriosis, I got pregnant last year, and my pregnancy and, now, breast-feeding appear to be doing what neither surgery nor the pill could—my cysts and lesions have disappeared, as has my chronic pain. If the disease doesn't recur, I'd like to stay away from synthetic hormones, especially since I get the occasional aura migraine, which means I have a higher risk for blood clots and stroke. If the endometriosis returns, however, a daily piece of duct tape on the dashboard light may be my best option.

"Knowing that most adverse events are rare, we must focus on the positives— first, family planning is good for women and families, and second, birth control methods provide many added benefits."

Let's Take a Moment to Talk About the Good Side Effects of Birth Control

Jessica Kiley

In the following viewpoint, Jessica Kiley argues that individuals should not allow sensational headlines and over-the-top political debates overshadow the health benefits of birth control. She says that because news stories and political debates about birth control all too often focus on the risks associated with the pill, people tend to become fixated on these real but rare health concerns and end up misled about how safe and beneficial the pill truly is. Kiley is a Chicago-based obstetrician-gynecologist and an assistant professor of obstetrics and gynecology at Northwestern University.

As you read, consider the following questions:

1. According to Kiley, 2014 marked the twentieth anniversary of what?

2. According to Kiley, women using birth control pills are at a lower risk for what cancers?

3. What does Kiley say are bad outcomes associated with birth control methods such as the pill?

If you take the control of birth control away from the legislators and the United States Supreme Court, diminish the politically charged conversations on women's health, and put in perspective sensational stories on contraception complications, what remains is the commonsense fact that birth control is a good thing.

Recently, a federal appeals court refused to allow the University of Notre Dame to deny insurance coverage for contraceptives to its students and employees. Claiming it countered the notion of religious freedom, a large retailer for airplane model kits and silk flowers filed a Supreme Court brief seeking exemption from the contraception mandate from the Department of Health and Human Services included in the Affordable Care Act. Hobby Lobby Stores, Inc. does not want employees in its 500 stores nationwide to have free access to 20 contraceptive options. And Catholic institutions such as the Little Sisters of the Poor Home for the Aged have also objected to the mandate and will have their day in court.

But none of these legal moves addresses the well-being of all women who want to maintain control of their reproductive health and experience the benefits of the good side effects of birth control.

Women who have planned pregnancies receive more prenatal care, and they have healthier pregnancies and healthier babies. Birth control allows women to achieve education and career goals, benefiting their families and society.

As 2014 marks the 20th anniversary of the United Nations' International Conference on Population and Development (the famous "Cairo conference"), it is time for America to lead by example with the best access to information on contraception for women. Too often, media attention turns to politics and the uncommon complications associated with birth control medications or devices, including a recent story on Essure, a call out from lawyers to prompt litigation on users of Yaz, and a release from the United Kingdom's National Health Service about birth control pills and blood clots.

These scare tactics are dangerous.

As a practicing obstetrician-gynecologist, I worry about the women who read these stories and shy away from using much-needed contraception. For more than 10 years I've taken care of women who safely use birth control.

These women have not only enjoyed protection from unplanned pregnancy, but they've also had the added benefit of something you rarely hear about—non-contraceptive benefits. These benefits are the "good side effects," which occur much more frequently than the bad ones that commonly make headlines.

A recent report from the Guttmacher Institute shows that abortion rates are the lowest in the United States since 1973. One contributing factor might be better access to birth control.

Pills are the most popular contraceptive in the United States, chosen by 27.5 percent of women who use some form of birth control. Oral contraceptives help regulate menstrual periods; women on standard birth control pills have predictable periods every 28 days. The positive side effects are lighter periods as well as less cramping and pain during menses.

Oral contraceptives are also commonly prescribed, specifically for relief of endometriosis and in controlling premenstrual dysphoric disorder. In addition, oral contraceptives have positive effects on skin and are effective for the treatment of acne.

Benefits are also seen in cancer prevention; women using birth control pills are at lower risk of developing cancers of the ovaries and endometrium. Since they are made of similar hormones and work much like birth control pills, contraceptive rings and patches are believed to deliver similar benefits.

More long-term contraception includes intrauterine devices, or IUDs, highly effective contraceptives that can last either five or 10 years, depending on the type. The five-year type, called the levonorgestrel intrauterine system, contains a hormone medication called a progestin, which is secreted directly into the uterus. Similar to birth control pills, this system provides relief of symptoms related to uterine fibroids and endometriosis. It can be a component of hormone replacement therapy for menopausal women.

Estrogen therapy in these women controls hot flushes, and the levonorgestrel IUD protects the uterus from overgrowing and possibly risking cancer. Furthermore, in certain women with precancers or cancers of the endometrium, the levonorgestrel IUD is an option for treatment of these conditions, and it is likely as effective as the standard oral medications used for decades.

The 10-year IUD contains a copper coil and no hormones. The lack of hormones alone is a major benefit to many women, who simply prefer an effective, hormone-free birth control option. Interestingly, some research shows that the copper IUD is associated with lower rates of endometrial cancer.

Other birth control methods containing progestins, such as the three-month shot and the three-year implant, also cause decreased menstrual bleeding. Women using the shot are very likely to stop having periods, a side effect they typically enjoy.

Critics will try to emphasize the severity of the bad outcomes, such as blood clots on pills or ring, or they may bring up bad events from decades ago, like pelvic infections with old IUDs no longer marketed. While this information is important, it should not guide the headlines or the discussions. Rare is rare, and history is history.

Non-contraceptive health benefits are clearly recognized by professional societies, such as the American Congress of Obstetricians and Gynecologists and the American Society for Reproductive Medicine, and these benefits must be threaded into our public conversations.

On a societal level, contraceptives need to be readily available for that primary reason—contraception. But we spend a lot of time talking about sensationally adverse events that don't happen to most women. And we spend a lot of time listening to political debate about reproductive rights.

In turn, women may view contraception as optional, or they may choose to not use birth control out of fear. Knowing that most adverse events are rare, we must focus on the positives—first, family planning is good for women and families, and second, birth control methods provide many added benefits.

Knowledge is power, and in this case, knowledge is also good health.

"Ultimately, even if one thinks that the prevention of fertilization is morally indifferent, surely it is not worth pursuing at the cost of innocent human life."

Emergency Contraception Is a Form of Abortion

Mathew Lu

In the following viewpoint, Mathew Lu argues that birth control is effectively a form of abortion. Specifically, Lu asserts that birth control methods that prevent the implantation of an embryo in the uterus lead to the death of a developing human. This, he says, is the functional equivalent of abortion and therefore morally reprehensible. Lu is an assistant professor of philosophy at the University of St. Thomas in St. Paul, Minnesota.

As you read, consider the following questions:

1. According to Lu, what can intelligibly be called "contraceptive"?

2. According to Lu, why is the pro-contraception argument about why birth control is not abortifacient flawed?

3. What really determines whether a particular type of birth control is an abortifacient, according to Lu?

One of the more controversial issues in the Supreme Court case concerning Hobby Lobby is the company's claim that some of the "emergency contraceptives" demanded by Obamacare [referring to the Patient Protection and Affordable Care Act] and the HHS [Department of Health and Human Services] mandate are actually "abortifacients" [agents that induce abortion]. The mainstream denial of this claim, supposedly backed by science, has largely revolved around a tendentious use of terms and a confusion about the real moral issues involved.

The defenders of emergency contraception, such as Guttmacher's Sneha Barot, like to claim that

> major medical organizations . . . as well as U.S. government policy, consider a pregnancy to have begun only when the entire process of conception is complete, which is to say after the fertilized egg has implanted in the lining of the uterus.

So, according to this putatively scientific definition, *conception* is distinct from fertilization, and *pregnancy* occurs only with the actual implanting of the embryo in the uterine lining. According to this definition of *conception*, anything that interferes with any part of this process, whether a physical barrier, hormonal regulation of ovulation (or sperm production), the destruction of the embryo prior to implantation, or prevention of successful implantation, can intelligibly be called *contraceptive.*

Similarly, if pregnancy only occurs once conception is complete with implantation, then it is intelligible to claim that abortion is best understood as the termination of a pregnancy—not the destruction of an embryo. This also explains the medical practice of calling early miscarriage "spontaneous abortion." Along these same lines, a method could only properly be called *abortifacient* insofar as it can cause (from the Latin *facio*) an abortion, which, in turn, is only possible after implantation.

These definitions allow emergency contraception advocates such as the Office of Population Research at Princeton University to make blanket assertions such as "There is no point in a woman's cycle when the emergency contraceptive pills available in the United States would end a *pregnancy* once it has started" (emphasis added). Using the definitions of *contraception* and *pregnancy* given above, that statement could very well be true, even if the "contraceptive pills" in question directly kill a living embryo or prevent its implantation.

The rhetoric sounds good. Emergency contraception does not prevent "pregnancy," therefore no "abortion" is involved, and no "abortifacient" methods are used.

However, this tendentious exercise in lexicography leads these advocates to confuse the real issue. Consider Sneha Barot's claim that

> if pregnancy were synonymous with the act of fertilization, all of the most effective reversible contraceptive methods—including oral contraceptive pills, injectables and IUDs—could be considered, at least theoretically, to be possible abortifacients.

Barot apparently takes it as obvious that these methods are not abortifacients, and therefore that pregnancy is not synonymous with fertilization. But, of course, whether some of these methods are abortifacients is exactly what's in question. It doesn't matter whether *pregnancy* is defined as synonymous with *fertilization*, but whether the methods in question directly kill an embryo or prevent its implantation.

The Principle of Double Effect

Ultimately, the moral question of abortion has little to do with the proper understanding of pregnancy at all. We can see this by reflecting on the fact that terminating a pregnancy is not evil *per se*. Any time a child is delivered by caesarian section, the pregnancy is terminated, but obviously there is no direct moral evil in that procedure. In fact, some pro-life moralists have even argued that some terminations of pregnancy are morally legitimate even if they result in the death of the child.

This line of argument makes use of the principle of double effect (PDE), which broadly holds that an act is morally permissible insofar as it meets four conditions (this formulation is derived from David Oderberg): (1) the intended effect of the act must not be intrinsically evil (e.g., aiming at the death of an innocent); (2) any evil side effects of the act must be unintended (though they may be foreseen); (3) the good intended effect must be at least as causally direct as any unintended side effect (i.e., one cannot do evil so that good may come of it); finally, (4) the intended good must be proportionate to any unintended evils (i.e., the good must "outweigh" the evil).

This method of moral reasoning has allowed some of these pro-life moralists to argue that in certain extreme circumstances it is morally permissible to terminate a pregnancy in a way that results in the death of the innocent child, so long as that death is not directly intended. Rarely, an embryo will implant within its mother's body outside the uterus (an ectopic pregnancy). While there have recently been extremely rare cases of ectopic pregnancy that were safely brought to birth (through caesarian section), it had traditionally been considered a death sentence for both the mother and child. For these reasons, some adherents of PDE have argued that it is permissible to remove the child surgically from the mother (intact) even though this foreseeably results in the death of the child. Simultaneously, these same moralists argue that the use of a chemical abortifacient to destroy the embryo is impermissible.

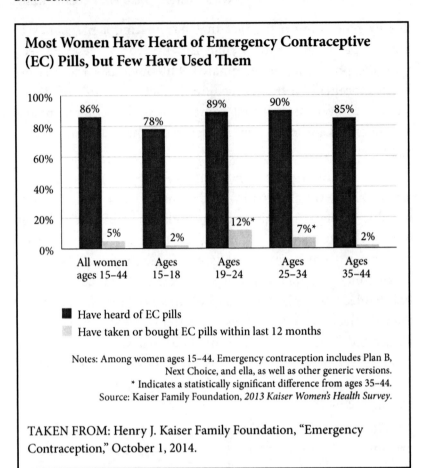

Most Women Have Heard of Emergency Contraceptive (EC) Pills, but Few Have Used Them

Have heard of EC pills

Have taken or bought EC pills within last 12 months

Notes: Among women ages 15–44. Emergency contraception includes Plan B, Next Choice, and ella, as well as other generic versions.
* Indicates a statistically significant difference from ages 35–44.
Source: Kaiser Family Foundation, *2013 Kaiser Women's Health Survey*.

TAKEN FROM: Henry J. Kaiser Family Foundation, "Emergency Contraception," October 1, 2014.

They reason that the surgical removal of the intact child is a medical treatment directly intended to save the mother's life. Killing the child is no part of that treatment (even as a means); were the technology available to save the child's life that would certainly be done. So the child's death is a foreseeable but unintended side effect of the surgery to treat the mother, and that foreseeable death is proportionate when weighed against the life of the mother. On the other hand, a chemical abortifacient would violate the PDE because, in treating the mother, the death of the child would be directly pursued. In other words, in the abortifacient case, the mother is being treated *by means of* killing the child. The child's death is not merely foreseen, it is actively pursued. That is also why the surgeon must remove the child intact; otherwise, the child's death would be directly pursued as a means.

Whether or not this particular analysis of ectopic pregnancy is ultimately correct, and we must be careful not to misuse the PDE as has sometimes been done, these examples clearly show that the moral defect of abortion lies not with the termination of the pregnancy, but with the direct killing of the child. In fact, one leading pro-life philosopher has argued that the ultimate solution to the abortion problem might lie in the technological development of artificial wombs. This would, at least in theory, allow the intact removal of "unwanted" embryos without necessarily resulting in their deaths.

If we return to the emergency contraception case, then it is apparent that the real issue is the mechanism by which they work, not what counts as pregnancy. While there are good reasons to think that contraception (understood merely as the prevention of fertilization) is itself morally defective, it is clearly a lesser evil than the destruction of an innocent human being. So I will mostly set the contraception question aside and focus on the destruction question.

The Unintended Evil: Killing an Innocent Human Being

On the one hand, the advocates of emergency contraception are quick to claim that "emergency contraceptive pills prevent pregnancy primarily, or perhaps exclusively, by delaying or inhibiting ovulation." Obviously, if no ovum is released, then fertilization is impossible. In that case, the moral concern is solely with contraception, not homicide. However, as Donna Harrison previously argued at *Public Discourse*, there are good empirical reasons to believe that some of the methods in question in the Hobby Lobby case [referring to *Burwell v. Hobby Lobby Stores*] "*can* and *do* cause embryos to die after fertilization."

It seems fair to say that the emergency contraception advocates' hedge that emergency contraception works "primarily, *or perhaps exclusively*, by delaying or inhibiting ovulation" (emphasis added) reflects lingering doubt about exactly how the methods work, even among those committed to promoting their use. This is a telling hesitation, a kind of residual honesty in admitting the possibility that, in at least some of the cases, these methods directly result in the death of embryos.... I suspect this hedging represents a kind of bad faith, and this in turn explains their repeated appeals to authority and attempts to take refuge in medical definitions of *pregnancy* and *abortion* that are morally irrelevant.

In the end, of course, none of the linguistic hairsplitting matters. What really matters in the morality of abortion is not whether a pregnancy has been terminated, but whether an innocent human being has been murdered. Understanding the mechanism of how these methods work is an empirical, scientific question about which there seems to be controversy within the medical community itself. However, I think it is significant that even the advocates of emergency contraception admit uncertainty about how the methods work and whether they kill embryos or prevent implantation.

From a moral perspective, if there is *any* plausible reason to believe that one of the consequences of the drugs is—even occasionally—the death of an embryo, then they are morally equivalent to abortifacients that work after implantation. The fact that the *intended* purpose of the drugs is to prevent ovulation is ultimately immaterial if their *actual consequence* is to kill living embryos or prevent implantation.

Ultimately, even if one thinks that the prevention of fertilization is morally indifferent, surely it is not worth pursuing at the cost of innocent human life. That is, it would not meet the proportionality requirement (4) of PDE. Furthermore, if contraception is itself an evil, then there is absolutely no good to set against even the possibility of killing an innocent human being, so proportionality would not even enter into it.

> "The assertion that women who use emergency contraceptives and IUDs (or even birth control pills and other hormonal methods) are in effect obtaining abortions is radical and far-reaching."

Emergency Contraception Is Not a Form of Abortion

Joerg Dreweke

In the following viewpoint, Joerg Dreweke argues that birth control is in no way a form of abortion. Citing scientific evidence that shows birth control prevents rather than ends pregnancy, Dreweke contends that those who paint contraception as abortifacient, or abortion causing, only do so as a means of furthering their antiabortion political agenda at the expense of women's rights and reproductive health rights. Dreweke is a senior policy communications associate with the Guttmacher Institute.

As you read, consider the following questions:

1. According to Dreweke, how do antiabortion groups pervert the science of contraception to promote their causes?

Joerg Dreweke, "Contraception Is Not Abortion: The Strategic Campaign of Antiabortion Groups to Persuade the Public Otherwise," *Guttmacher Policy Review*, 2014, 17(4):14–20. Copyright © 2014 The Guttmacher Institute. All rights reserved. Reproduced with permission.

2. What is one of the few antiabortion groups that opposes contraception outright, according to the viewpoint?

3. According to Dreweke, what are antiabortion groups really aiming to do by claiming that some forms of birth control are abortifacient?

Among the many storylines coming out of the November 2014 midterm elections are two centered on birth control. American voters decisively rejected ballot measures in two states that sought to define human personhood—with all its attendant legal rights—as starting at fertilization. This "personhood" agenda seeks not just to ban abortion, but some common Food and Drug Administration (FDA)–approved contraceptive methods as well, because personhood proponents assert that these methods work by preventing implantation of a fertilized egg. At the same time, conservative candidates did well at the ballot box, in part, by keeping mum about or obfuscating their positions that would undermine access to birth control—for instance, by removing insurance coverage for contraceptive services.

The underlying lesson—that the "personhood" movement's perceived frontal assault on birth control is a political non-starter—has apparently not been lost on prominent U.S. antiabortion groups like Americans United for Life (AUL), Susan B. Anthony List (SBA List), the Heritage Foundation and the U.S. Conference of Catholic Bishops (USCCB). These mainstays of the U.S. antiabortion movement have sought to keep their distance, at least publicly, from fights over personhood amendments, even as they work in myriad ways to undermine access to contraception.

Yet, these same mainstream antiabortion groups have not shied away from asserting in other contexts that certain methods of contraception are actually methods of abortion. They have in effect selectively embraced the core "personhood" argument—that U.S. policy should in some circumstances recognize pregnancy as beginning at fertilization—as a way to undermine access to birth control. That strategy reached a new high-water mark when it featured centrally in *Burwell v. Hobby Lobby*, the high-profile 2014 U.S. Supreme Court case that granted certain for-profit employers an exemption from the [Patient Protection and] Affordable Care Act's (ACA's) contraceptive coverage guarantee. During this debate, leading organizations dedicated to banning abortion unequivocally endorsed the view—in legal briefs, press statements and elsewhere—that emergency contraceptives and IUDs [intrauterine devices] constitute abortion.

The contrast between these two policy debates highlights something critically important but often overlooked about much of the antiabortion movement. Birth control is very much in the movement's crosshairs, and antiabortion advocates are working to stigmatize contraception by blurring the lines between contraception and abortion. Yet, the movement is doing this in a strategic and deceptive way. Rather than applying the claim that some contraceptive methods in effect cause abortion consistently to all aspects of their advocacy, antiabortion groups ignore and often contradict their positions when it might hurt them politically. Taking the antiabortion movement at face value by consistently treating some forms of contraception as abortifacients—including under federal and state law—would expose how radical their agenda truly is and would have far-reaching implications for women who obtain contraceptive services and providers who offer them.

The Science

The campaign to conflate contraception with abortion is based on the assertion that certain methods of contraception actually end—rather than prevent—pregnancy. That assertion, however, contradicts what science says about how pregnancies are established and how contraceptives work. These facts are laid out in detail in an amicus brief submitted to the Supreme

Court in October 2013 by numerous medical associations, led by Physicians for Reproductive Health and the American College of Obstetricians and Gynecologists. A contraceptive method, by definition, prevents pregnancy by interfering with ovulation, fertilization or implantation. Abortion ends an established pregnancy, after implantation. This scientific definition of pregnancy—which reflects the fact that most fertilized eggs naturally fail to implant in the uterus—is also the legal definition, and has long been accepted by federal agencies (during administrations both supportive of and opposed to abortion rights), and by U.S. and international medical associations.

The amicus brief describes the most up-to-date evidence about how hormonal and copper IUDs and the emergency contraceptives Plan B and ella work, and documents that none have been shown to disrupt an existing pregnancy—meaning that none can accurately be called an abortifacient. Rather, both Plan B and ella work primarily by preventing ovulation; they can work for up to five days after sex, because sperm can survive in a woman's body for that long. Both the hormonal and copper IUDs work primarily by preventing sperm from reaching and fertilizing an egg. Of all these methods, only the copper IUD, when used as an emergency contraceptive, appears capable of preventing implantation of a fertilized egg. However, even then it would not be considered an abortion under standard medical and legal definitions.

The weight of the evidence clearly shows that emergency contraceptives and IUDs are not abortifacients. And yet, the science, when marshaled in bad faith and combined with anti-contraception activists' redefining pregnancy as beginning with fertilization, provides them with ambiguity to exploit. The antiabortion movement has a long history of strategically using outdated information and outright junk science to restrict access to reproductive health care, from the supposed mental health impact of abortion to discredited assertions that abortion causes breast cancer.

The medical groups' amicus brief illustrates this approach by highlighting the anti-contraception movement's reliance on outdated FDA product labels to implicate Plan B. While the label states that Plan B "may inhibit implantation (by altering the endometrium)," the brief notes that this "label has not been updated since the product was originally approved in 1999 and it does not reflect the most current research." Rather, "later studies have led to the conclusion that [Plan B] does not cause changes to the endometrium (uterine lining) that would hamper implantation." However, updating FDA-approved labels is a time-consuming and expensive process for both the agency and the relevant drug company, so it is not uncommon that such labels do not keep pace with the underlying science.

More so, the FDA labeling for some popular forms of birth control pills contains similar statements. For instance, while the labels for the combined oral contraceptive pills Yaz and Yasmin say that they work primarily by suppressing ovulation, they also state that "other possible mechanisms may include . . . endometrial changes that reduce the likelihood of implantation." However, mainstream antiabortion groups, in contrast to the "personhood" movement, appear to have long concluded that a frontal assault on the pill—the most popular reversible form of contraception, with more than 10 million current users—would be a sure political loser. That is why their attacks have focused on less commonly used methods, like IUDs and emergency contraceptives.

Having It Both Ways

Conflating contraception with abortion as a means to chip away at contraceptive access is not a new approach, but the debate over the ACA's contraceptive coverage guarantee has given it a new prominence. That this guarantee, even though it explicitly extends only to FDA-approved contraceptive methods, requires private insurance plans to cover abortion is gospel among virtually every influential antiabortion group. AUL states that the policy is a "backdoor abortion mandate" that requires employers to cover "life-ending drugs that have been deceptively labeled as contraception." SBA List also refers to the guarantee as an "Abortion Drug Mandate," while the Heritage Foundation says it requires "coverage of abortion-inducing drugs and devices."

Court briefs filed by various antiabortion groups in support of Hobby Lobby's refusal to cover certain contraceptives assert that the case is about the company's right to refuse on religious grounds to facilitate abortion. A brief signed by SBA List says the ACA policy "directly intrudes on the choice not to participate in abortion." The brief from USCCB contains numerous references to objecting companies being forced to cover "abortion-inducing drugs and devices."

Echoing the Hobby Lobby complaint, antiabortion groups have zeroed in on emergency contraceptives and IUDs as causing abortions. SBA List has routinely referred to emergency contraceptives as "abortion drugs" and describes the copper IUD as causing "early abortion." The American Association of Pro-Life Obstetricians and Gynecologists (AAPLOG) says that Plan B can lead to "embryo death" by preventing implantation and that "IUDs work by either killing the embryo or by preventing the embryo from implanting." And AUL asserts that IUDs and Plan B "can kill an embryo by blocking its ability to implant in the uterus."

Many of these groups also assert—contrary to the best available evidence—that the emergency contraceptive ella has a postimplantation effect. For instance, AUL claims that "ella can kill an embryo even after implantation has occurred," a position that is echoed by USCCB and AAPLOG, among others.

Despite their forceful and sustained assertions while debating the ACA's contraceptive coverage guarantee that emergency contraceptives and IUDs constitute abortion, groups like AUL, SBA List and USCCB simply pretend in other contexts that they hold no such views. For instance, when discussing abortion incidence statistics, they accept without question the mainstream definition of abortion as ending an established (that is, postimplantation) pregnancy. A good example is a February 2014 article by USCCB's Richard Doerflinger discussing the decline in U.S. abortion rates. Doerflinger consistently refers to IUDs and emergency contraception as "contraceptives" or "contraception," never mentioning these methods' supposed abortifacient qualities and accepting without question (and contrary to the bishops' own position) the mainstream definition of abortion as the termination of an established pregnancy.

The same goes for these groups' efforts to enact antiabortion legislation. Despite their significant legislative and lobbying clout, they have not made the case that emergency contraceptives and IUDs should be treated as causing abortion for purposes such as legislating waiting periods, onerous clinic facilities requirements, parental consent requirements or mandates that only physicians may provide the service.

This tactic is deceptive and disingenuous on multiple levels: The claim that some contraceptives cause abortion is based both on a nonscientific definition of pregnancy and on outdated information including FDA labels that have not kept pace with newer research. At the same time, this definition and outdated science are applied inconsistently to some methods, but not others—most notably omitting various forms of birth control pills. Lastly, these supposedly "abortion-inducing drugs and devices" are entirely exempted from the rest of these groups' extensive antiabortion agenda. This wildly inconsistent and cynical approach seems grounded in political expediency and can only serve one purpose: to obscure these groups' full antiabortion and anti-contraception agenda.

Far-Reaching Implications

Under current federal and state laws and regulations, for the most part, it is clear that abortion and contraception are separate from each other. And for their part, the influential antiabortion groups that have been conflating some contraceptives with abortion have been mostly silent on whether existing abortion laws should apply to these contraceptives.

One notable exception is from an October 2014 comment letter to the U.S. Department of Health and Human Services regarding implementation of the ACA contraceptive coverage guarantee, in which the USCCB asserts that specific federal and state abortion restrictions concerning insurance coverage of abortion should apply to the emergency contraceptive ella. To argue, as the USCCB unequivocally does, that an FDA-approved method of contraception should be treated as an abortifacient under federal and state abortion law is truly radical. It is also somewhat surprising because the USCCB is one of the few major antiabortion organizations that unequivocally opposes contraception outright (other than periodic abstinence within marriage), obviating the need to hide behind making a case that certain birth control methods are really forms of abortion.

If a particular federal or state abortion restriction should apply to this method of contraception, then there is no reason why the gamut of federal and state abortion restrictions should not apply to it as well—or, for that matter, why all abortion policies should not apply to any method that antiabortion groups consider to cause abortion. The USCCB seems well aware of the implications of its views, expressing them only in obscure comment letters, but omitting them in more high-profile settings.

Emergency Contraception

Regular use of hormonal contraception prevents ovulation and the chance for fertilization: emergency contraception essentially works the same way except that it's taken after sex, by which point ovulation may have already happened. But according to recent studies, there is no evidence that taking emergency contraception after ovulation and fertilization will stop the egg from implanting.

Irin Carmon,
"The Myth of the 'Morning After Birth Control Pill,'"
Salon, April 26, 2012.

There are hundreds of policies in effect that regulate and restrict access to abortion care across the United States, both at the federal and, especially, the state level. Treating some contraceptives as abortifacients and applying the full range of existing abortion restrictions to them would have a dramatic impact. In many cases, the outcome would border on the ridiculous—demonstrating just how out of touch the campaign to define certain contraceptives as causing abortion really is.

Implications for Women

If the myriad hardships and indignities to which U.S. women who obtain abortions are often subjected were applied to IUD and emergency contraceptive users, the effect would border on the bizarre. A woman seeking to purchase emergency contraceptives in Mississippi, for example, would need to make an initial trip to the provider to first undergo mandatory in-person counseling, as well as a mandatory ultrasound exam. She would then have to wait a minimum of 24 hours before making the second trip to obtain the emergency contraceptives. If she were insured through Medicaid, her insurance would be prohibited from covering the cost of the method. If she were a legal minor, she would need the consent of both parents.

Defining some contraceptives as abortifacients could even put women who use these methods in legal jeopardy. For instance, women who self-administer Plan B would potentially run afoul of state laws that prohibit self-inducing an abortion or practicing medicine without a license.

Implications for Providers

Pharmacists, clinicians and others who sell emergency contraceptives, insert IUDs or otherwise make available birth control methods that antiabortion groups consider to cause abortion would be affected in numerous ways. The most far-reaching impact would stem from the Targeted Regulation of Abortion Providers (TRAP). If these policies applied, a physician in Missouri inserting an IUD would be required to do so in an ambulatory surgical center and would also need hospital admitting privileges.

Numerous other abortion laws would come into play as well, including reporting requirements in effect in 46 states. If emergency contraceptives and IUDs were "abortion-inducing drugs and devices," it is unclear how these supposed abortions should or could be counted and, for that matter, how many "abortions" by this definition would actually be induced in the United States each year. Two of the most extreme openly anti-contraception groups, the American Life League and Pharmacists for Life [International], have asserted that the "real" number of U.S. abortions—including those supposedly caused by contraceptives—is four to five times higher than what is currently counted.

Implications Going Forward

The anti-contraception movement's efforts in the past several years have focused on rolling back the ACA's provision that most private health plans must cover contraceptive services, counseling and methods without out-of-pocket costs. This campaign scored a significant victory with the Supreme Court's *Hobby Lobby* decision, an outgrowth of dozens of court cases pursuing exemptions from the ACA guarantee for for-profit and nonprofit organizations that have religious or moral objections to some or all contraceptives. The movement also supports repealing the entire ACA and has aggressively pursued that agenda legislatively, electorally and through the courts.

An emerging, although still fringe, frontier in the campaign to curtail contraceptive access appears to be the attempted restriction of public insurance coverage (under Medicaid and other federal or state programs) and other public funding for some contraceptive methods by claiming they cause abortion. Attacks on funding for contraception, such as funding for the Title X national family planning program, are by no means new, but they have typically taken an indirect approach—for example, by complaining that providing public funding to family planning centers "frees up" centers' private funding to be used for abortion care. In 2014, however, Colorado gubernatorial candidate Bob Beauprez (R) stated his opposition to any public funding for IUDs on the grounds that the "IUD is an abortifacient." And in Kansas, a county rejected a $6,000 grant for contraceptives from the state health department after one commissioner "likened intrauterine devices to murder."

The Real Agenda

The assertion that women who use emergency contraceptives and IUDs (or even birth control pills and other hormonal methods) are in effect obtaining abortions is radical and far-reaching. It is not supported by the science, nor by mainstream medical groups. And it is completely out of step with Americans' attitudes toward contraception and the actions of tens of millions of U.S. women and couples who use birth control to prevent pregnancy, not end it.

The influential organizations behind this anti-contraception agenda have compartmentalized the debate, which allows them to pick and choose when contraception should be viewed as abortion and when it should not. They are essentially able to pursue a "personhood" argument in areas where doing so is politically feasible, but at the same time feign moderation by keeping the full-fledged, politically toxic "personhood" agenda at arm's length. This deception is part of a deliberate, long-term strategy to limit women's access not only to safe and legal abortion, but to common methods of contraception as well.

Reproductive health and rights advocates, the media and the public at large need to recognize that the full underlying agenda against reproductive rights is far-reaching, even if sometimes somewhat veiled. In that light, current battles over the ACA's contraceptive coverage guarantee reflect a fundamental public policy chasm that pits those wanting to restrict women's health care choices against those who want to protect and expand them. Antiabortion groups are trying to coerce women's reproductive decision making by restricting access not only to abortion services, but by undermining private insurance coverage of contraceptives, defunding publicly supported family planning services and opposing comprehensive sex education, among other tactics. This approach stands in stark contrast to that supported by reproductive rights advocates, who have long pushed for policies grounded in voluntarism and informed consent that support all of a woman's pregnancy decisions.

When organizations whose core mission is to ban abortion say that some contraceptives are abortion, then their obvious intent is to eventually ban these methods. They are not neutral on the issue of contraception, despite their protestations to the contrary. Contraception is not abortion, however. If those who believe and insist otherwise have the courage to own up to their beliefs publicly and consistently, then the full breadth of their anti–reproductive health and rights agenda will be plain for all to see.

Periodical and Internet Sources Bibliography

The following articles have been selected to supplement the diverse views presented in this chapter.

Jessica Arons	"Untapped Potential of the Abortion Pill, 15 Years Later," *The Hill*, October 1, 2015.
Laura Bassett	"Over-the-Counter Birth Control May Be a Game-Changer," *Huffington Post*, February 27, 2015.
Elizabeth Nolan Brown	"Over-the-Counter Birth Control Pills? Not in America," *Reason*, March 26, 2014.
Lauren Enriquez	"Studies Show All Forms of Emergency Contraception Cause Abortion," Live Action News, April 30, 2014.
Casey Gueren	"How Worried Should You REALLY Be About All Those Birth Control Risks?," *Women's Health*, August 21, 2014.
Jamie Hergenrader	"The Dangerous Side of Birth Control," *Huffington Post*, July 31, 2013.
Barbara Feder Ostrov	"Calif., Ore. Allow Women to Get Birth Control Without a Prescription," *USA Today*, July 12, 2015.
Amelia Thomson-Deveaux	"Offering Birth Control Over the Counter Wouldn't Make It Any Cheaper," *FiveThirtyEight*, November 18, 2014.
Sarah Watts	"An Over-the-Counter Pill Isn't Safe," Daily Beast, June 15, 2015.
Susan Wills	"New Studies Show All Emergency Contraceptives Can Cause Early Abortion," Charlotte Lozier Institute, January 1, 2014.

OPPOSING
VIEWPOINTS®
SERIES

Chapter 4

What Are the Social Consequences of Using Birth Control?

Chapter Preface

While the ongoing birth control conversation is often dominated by questions such as whether some contraceptives are the equivalent of abortion or whether employers should be required to cover the cost of contraceptives, it also encompasses some broader societal issues. Some of these issues include the role birth control accessibility plays in the abortion rate and the impact of birth control on population growth. Another is the effect birth control might be having on the environment.

Hormone-based forms of contraception, such as the birth control pill, contain a synthetic estrogen called 17α-ethinyl estradiol, or EE2. Recent studies have shown that EE2 and other synthetic estrogens are being leached into water sources where they have a harmful effect on aquatic life-forms. Specifically, these chemicals interfere with the reproductive abilities of fish and amphibians, sometimes even causing them to develop both male and female sexual organs and traits. There is also concern that humans who consume water contaminated with these synthetic estrogens may also be at risk of hormonal imbalances and reproductive dysfunction. Indeed, some studies have confirmed that there has been an increase in human fertility issues tied to the existence of synthetic estrogens in the environment. For anti–birth control advocates, this revelation is further proof of the inherent dangers of contraceptives and yet another reason to abandon their use.

Birth control supporters, however, argue that to lay the blame for synthetic estrogen pollution solely or even mostly on contraceptives is inaccurate and irresponsible. They point out that birth control is only one of many sources of synthetic estrogen and the environmental pollution that results from its use. In fact, thousands of different synthetic estrogens are actually found in a wide variety of products such as industrial chemicals, fertilizers, and livestock feed. From the perspective of birth control advocates, blaming birth control for synthetic estrogen pollution is little more than a thinly veiled attempt to demonize birth control itself and distract the public from the more prominent industrial sources of such chemicals. They argue that when addressing pollution problems of this sort, it is imperative to keep both environmental and reproductive health needs in mind.

Because the use of birth control is a social issue, it is also an issue that will always have societal implications on regional, national, and even global levels. The following chapter examines some of the societal consequences of using birth control, including abortion rates and environmental risk.

> "When price wasn't an issue, women flocked to the most effective contraceptives—the implanted options, which typically cost hundreds of dollars up front to insert. These women experienced far fewer unintended pregnancies as a result."

Birth Control Does Not Lead to More Abortions

Associated Press

In the following viewpoint, the Associated Press (AP) reports on a study indicating that the use of birth control leads to fewer incidences of abortion. The AP touches on both the study itself and the role contraception plays in the Patient Protection and Affordable Care Act, also known as Obamacare. Ultimately, the AP makes a compelling argument in support of birth control as a means to prevent abortions. The Associated Press is a New York–based nonprofit multinational news agency.

As you read, consider the following questions:

1. According to the AP, how many abortions could be prevented for every 79 to 137 women given free contraception?

2. Why is birth control an important public health issue, according to the viewpoint?

3. According to the AP, what percentage of women in the United States choose long-acting contraceptives?

Free birth control led to dramatically lower rates of abortions and teen births, a large study concluded Thursday [October 4, 2012]. The findings were eagerly anticipated and come as a bitterly contested [Barack] Obama administration policy is poised to offer similar coverage.

What the Study Reveals

The project tracked more than 9,000 women in St. Louis, many of them poor or uninsured. They were given their choice of a range of contraceptive methods at no cost—from birth control pills to goof-proof options like the IUD [intrauterine device] or a matchstick-sized implant.

When price wasn't an issue, women flocked to the most effective contraceptives—the implanted options, which typically cost hundreds of dollars up front to insert. These women experienced far fewer unintended pregnancies as a result, reported Dr. Jeffrey Peipert of Washington University in St. Louis in a study published Thursday.

The effect on teen pregnancy was striking: There were 6.3 births per 1,000 teenagers in the study. Compare that to a national rate of 34 births per 1,000 teens in 2010.

There also were substantially lower rates of abortion, when compared with women in the metro area and nationally: 4.4 to 7.5 abortions per 1,000 women in the study, compared with 13.4 to 17 abortions per 1,000 women overall in the St. Louis region, Peipert calculated. That's lower than the national rate, too, which is almost 20 abortions per 1,000 women.

Progress in Reducing Unplanned Pregnancy and Abortion

Family planning is an effective way to prevent unplanned pregnancy—and because well over 90% of abortions are sought in the wake of an unplanned pregnancy, family planning also reduces abortion. This is particularly true among unmarried women, who are more likely than married women to terminate an unplanned pregnancy. In fact, only one in 20 unplanned pregnancies occur among women who were using contraception correctly and consistently.

Kelleen Kaye, Jennifer Appleton Gootman,
Alison Stewart Ng, and Cara Finley,
"The Benefits of Birth Control in America:
Getting the Facts Straight," National Campaign to
Prevent Teen and Unplanned Pregnancy, June 2014.

In fact, if the program were expanded, one abortion could be prevented for every 79 to 137 women given a free contraceptive choice, Peipert's team reported in the journal *Obstetrics & Gynecology*.

Birth Control and Obamacare

The findings of the study, which ran from 2008 to 2010, come as millions of U.S. women are beginning to get access to contraception without co-pays under President Obama's health care law [referring to the Patient Protection and Affordable Care Act, also known as Obamacare]. Women's health specialists said the research foreshadows that policy's potential impact.

"As a society, we want to reduce unintended pregnancies and abortion rates. This study has demonstrated that having access to no-cost contraception helps us get to that goal," said Alina Salganicoff, director of women's health policy at the [Henry J.] Kaiser Family Foundation.

"It's just an amazing improvement," Dr. James T. Breeden, president of the American Congress of Obstetricians and Gynecologists, said of the results. "I would think if you were against abortions, you would be 100 percent for contraception access."

The law requires that Food and Drug Administration [FDA]–approved contraceptives be available for free for women enrolled in most workplace insurance plans, a change that many will see as new plan years begin on Jan. 1 [2013].

The policy is among the law's most contentious provisions because it exempts churches that oppose contraception but requires religious-affiliated organizations, such as colleges or hospitals, to provide the coverage for their workers. The U.S. Conference of Catholic Bishops and many conservative groups say that violates religious freedom, and Republican presidential nominee Mitt Romney has voiced similar criticism.

This week, a federal judge in St. Louis dismissed a lawsuit challenging the contraception mandate; nearly three dozen similar suits have been filed around the country.

Thursday's data didn't sway the critics.

Jeanne Monahan of the conservative Family Research Council suggested contraceptive use can encourage riskier sexual behavior.

"Additionally, one might conclude that the Obama administration's contraception mandate may ultimately cause more unplanned pregnancies since it mandates that all health plans cover contraceptives, including those that the study's authors claim are less effective," Monahan said.

The Truth About Birth Control

Here's why this is a public health issue: Nearly half of the nation's 6 million-plus pregnancies each year are unintended.

An estimated 43 percent of them end in abortion. Low-income women are far more likely to have an unplanned pregnancy than their wealthier counterparts.

"We shouldn't have, in my view, a tiered system where the women with money can get family planning and the women without cannot," said Peipert, noting that 39 percent of the women in his study had trouble paying basic expenses.

About half of unplanned pregnancies occur in women who use no contraception. As for the other half, condoms can fail and so can birth control pills or other shorter-acting methods if the woman forgets to use them or can't afford a refill.

In contrast, you can forget about pregnancy for three years with Implanon, the implant inserted under the skin of the arm. An IUD, a tiny T-shaped device inserted into the uterus, can last for five to 10 years, depending on the brand. Change your mind, and the doctor removes either device before it wears out.

Only about 5 percent of U.S. women use long-acting contraceptives, far fewer than in other developed countries. Peipert said insurance hasn't always covered the higher up-front cost to insert them, even though years of birth control pills can add up to the same price.

Yet, three-quarters of his study participants chose an IUD or Implanon, and a year later 85 percent were sticking to that choice—compared to about half who had initially chosen the pill, patch or other shorter-acting method.

Cost isn't the only barrier. Doctors don't always mention long-acting methods, maybe because of a long-outdated belief that IUDs aren't for young women or just because they assume women want the most commonly prescribed pill.

That was the case for Ashley England, 26, of Nashville, Tenn., who enrolled in the study while in graduate school in St. Louis. She had taken birth control pills for years but struggled with a $50 monthly co-pay. She switched to a five-year IUD, and loves that she and her husband don't have to think about contraception.

"No one had ever presented all the options equally," England said. "It's not telling you what to do. It's giving you a choice unhindered by money."

> *"In the final analysis, the strategy of promoting more contraceptive use to decrease abortion approaches the textbook definition of insanity: doing the same thing over and over again and expecting different results."*

Birth Control Leads to More Abortions

Peter Baklinski

In the following viewpoint, Peter Baklinski argues that the use of birth control only serves to increase the abortion rate. In the course of his argument, Baklinski decries birth control, claiming that it is the lynchpin in what he calls the "'get rich quick' scheme of the multibillion-dollar abortion industry," and, effectively, a form of abortion in and of itself. Further, he adds that contraception is a deep-seated moral evil that must be removed for society to flourish. Baklinski is a journalist with LifeSiteNews and an expert in theology.

As you read, consider the following questions:

1. According to Baklinski, how does the Catholic Church teach that couples can postpone pregnancy?

2. What role does abortion play in a society that embraces contraception, according to the viewpoint?

3. According to Baklinski, how does contraception change the meaning of sex?

A pro-life atheist from the Maritimes argued last week [in April 2013] that the Catholic Church's teaching against contraception undermines its argument against abortion. But had he examined recent research on the matter as well as looked into the abortifacient [abortion causing] mechanism built into mainstream contraceptives, he might have reached a different conclusion.

Jackson Doughart, a political theorist student at Queen's University, wrote in the *National Post* on Wednesday that a "prohibition on contraceptives would doubtless result in many undesired pregnancies, and hence a greater number of candidates for abortion."

The Catholic Church teaches that "each and every marriage act must remain open to the transmission of human life," and thereby excludes "every action ... to render procreation impossible." The church also teaches that a couple can naturally and morally postpone pregnancy by not having sex during the woman's fertile period.

Doughart's piece, titled *The Vatican's Opposition to Contraception Undermines Fight Against Abortion*, was a response to a correspondent who had privately attempted to convince the atheist that the church's teaching against contraception "makes her position entirely consistent." The correspondent, who held in high esteem Doughart's secular defense for the right to life of the unborn, suggested that the defense could be tightened "if you found a way to reason to why [the unborn] face this plight in the first place."

In an attempt to shed light on the church's position, the unnamed correspondent wrote to Doughart: "*Contraception closes the sexual act to the gift of life. Once a contracepting man and woman have allowed a contraceptive mentality to seep into them, they immediately view a newly created child as an inconvenience at best and as a hostile intruder at worst. For them, the only solution is to get rid of the baby through abortion. You see, contraception leads to the need for abortion."*

But Doughart called the claim "absurd" that "Sexual Act A, which is performed with contraception, is more likely to result in abortion than Sexual Act B, which is performed without."

Echoing the oft-used pro-contraception argument of the abortion giant Planned Parenthood [Federation of America,] Doughart concluded: "I don't see how both a practicable and philosophically defensible argument against contraception can be made by anyone who is genuinely interested in reducing abortion."

Abortion Advocates Link Contraception to Abortion

But adamant abortion advocates don't agree with Doughart's conclusion, pointing out that a link does indeed exist between contraception and demand for abortion.

"Most abortions result from failed contraception," admitted Joyce Arthur, founder and executive director of the Abortion Rights Coalition of Canada, earlier this year.

Arthur's statement parallels a prediction made in 1973 by Dr. Malcolm Potts, former medical director of the International Planned Parenthood Federation, who said: "As people turn to contraception, there will be a rise, not a fall, in the abortion rate."

What Arthur and Potts have perhaps unwittingly revealed is the massively lucrative 'get rich quick' scheme of the multibillion-dollar abortion industry: 1) encourage unrestricted sexual activity among young people; 2) promote the idea of "safe sex" without consequences especially through using contraception; 3) expect contraception to fail since every method, be it the condom, pill, intrauterine device [IUD], etc., has a startlingly dismal failure rate in real world usage; and 4) provide abortions to women as a solution to their 'unexpected problem.'

Researchers have exposed this ingenious business plan of the abortion industry simply by following the money. They found that contraception is the gateway mechanism for increasing abortion. And abortion is where the profit is.

Analysts have exposed the abortion-centered nature in the case of Planned Parenthood's business model, finding in the organization's own billion-dollar financial reports that abortions account for more than half its income.

Experts Say Contraception Necessitates Abortion

The United States' highest court had no difficulty in seeing the causal link between contraception and abortion in a 1992 ruling that confirmed *Roe v. Wade*, the 1973 decision that brought legal abortion to America.

In *Planned Parenthood v. Casey*, the Supreme Court argued that in some critical respects abortion is of the same character as the decision to use contraception: ". . . for two decades of economic and social developments, [people] have organized intimate relationships and made choices that define their views of themselves and their places in society, in reliance on the availability of abortion in the event that contraception should fail."

What the Supreme Court pointed out is that in a contracepting society, abortion not only becomes a necessity, but it becomes the ultimate fail-safe method of birth control. In the mind of the court, contraception doesn't lessen the need for abortion, but on the contrary, contraception precipitates abortion.

One woman, writing at the pro-abortion website RH RealityCheck.com last year, expressed her bewilderment at the failure of her intrauterine device. Confirming the validity of what the Supreme Court said, she described the process that led her to "fix" the problem by having her baby aborted.

"Something went wrong, but now there are steps to fix it," wrote the woman who identified herself as NW. "Yes, I'm pregnant, but it's a temporary state. I can see the day on the calendar when it won't be true anymore."

"I go with Planned Parenthood," writes NW. "I spend so much of my time defending them and giving money monthly, it seems only right to maintain my loyalty in my moment of need."

Dr. Dianne Irving, a bioethicist at Georgetown University and a former bench biochemist with the U.S. National Institutes of Health, would have no trouble explaining NW's series of choices that led to the demise of her growing baby.

"Since it is . . . a long-recognized and documented scientific fact that almost all so-called 'contraceptives' routinely fail at statistically significant rates resulting in 'unplanned pregnancies,' is there any wonder that elective abortions are socially required in order to take care of such 'accidents?'" Dr. Irving asked.

"Thus abortion has become a 'contraceptive' in and of itself," she said.

Dr. Janet Smith, a professor, author, and national speaker, agrees with Dr. Irving: "Contraception leads us to believe that sex can be a momentary encounter, not a life-long commitment. It has brought about the concept of 'accidental pregnancy.'"

"The connection between contraception and abortion is primarily this: Contraception facilitates the kind of relationships and even the kind of attitudes and moral characters that are likely to lead to abortion," she wrote.

Put differently, contraception radically changes the meaning and purpose of sex. Contraception turns the sexual act between a man and a woman that is biologically ordered toward the creation of a new life into a parody of the act, where a

The Truth About Contraception and Abortion

The results are in: Contraception availability does not reduce unintended pregnancies.

Many adolescent males will wholeheartedly affirm a connection between the availability of contraception and sexual activity, and scientific data supports the link. Studies have shown that contraception increases sexual activity—i.e., that more contraception means more sex.

Keith Riler, "Studies: Birth Control, Contraception Don't Cut Abortions," LifeNews.com, February 17, 2012.

newly created life can suddenly be viewed as an uninvited and unwelcome guest. Abortion becomes the easy solution by which the parent permanently and violently disinvites the unwelcome guest.

Sarah Nelson is one woman who discovered within her own heart that her acceptance of contraception instilled in her what she called a "spirit of abortion." Sarah always considered herself to be pro-life, but she was also in favor of contraception. She had been raised among Protestants who openly encouraged newlyweds to contracept.

"Rarely were children talked about in terms of 'abundance and overflowing joy,'" she said. Some of her mentors strongly suggested that couples should limit their family size "for the good of God."

One day after praying for an end to abortion on the anniversary of *Roe v. Wade*, Sarah became aware of an anti-life mentality that had insidiously rooted itself deep within her. She saw that this mentality had prejudiced her against valuing new human life and that it was responsible for blocking her own desire one day to have children of her own. She realized that this mentality came from her uncritical acceptance of contraception.

"I was not really open to having children, nor had I been encouraged to be so from my church leadership," she said. "From this flowed the natural conclusion that contraception was fine. And if contraception was fine, then I could see how the logic worked that allowed abortion (God forbid) to be fine because it got rid of an 'inconvenience,'" she said.

"I was horrified as I suddenly and instantly knew the horrible truth: being closed to life through contraception actually leads to the reality and horror of abortion," she said.

High Contraception Rates Increase Abortion Rates

Research backs up the causal link between contraception and abortion.

A 2011 Spanish study found that as use of contraceptive methods increased in a sample of more than 2000 Spanish women (49.1% to 79.9%), the rate of abortion in the group doubled in the same period.

The researchers were clearly puzzled by the findings of their 10-year study, calling it "interesting and paradoxical" that the large increase in elective abortions was associated with a remarkable increase in the number of women who used contraceptive methods.

Research from the pro-abortion Guttmacher Institute showed in 2011 that a majority of abortions took place in America after contraception failure: "54 percent of women who have abortions had used a contraceptive method [usually condom or the pill] during the month they became pregnant."

The former Planned Parenthood associate also found that "[p]oor women's high rate of unintended pregnancy results in their also having high—and increasing—rates of both abortions (52 per 1,000) and unplanned births (66 per 1,000)."

A 2012 Russian study found that while Russian women had the highest rate of contraceptive use when compared to surrounding countries, they also had the highest abortion rate.

The researchers were clearly perplexed when they found "higher odds of modern contraception" led to a "higher level of abortion," calling their findings "contradictory," "unexpected," and "paradoxical."

Like the researchers in the Russian study, Swedish officials were baffled earlier this year by statistics showing a rise in the country's abortion rate following the introduction of the abortifacient morning-after pill. Despite sales in the pill having doubled between 2001 and 2012, the abortion rate approximately within the same period was seen to have increased from 18.4 to 20.9 per 1,000 women.

"Our hope was that the pill would bring down the abortion rates," said Catharina Zätterström, deputy chairwoman at the Swedish Association of Midwives.

Mainstream Contraceptives Have Killed Millions

Doughart's essential argument that contraception ought to make sense to "anyone who is genuinely interested in reducing abortion" appears logical at first glance, until it is pointed out that mainstream methods of contraception—such as the pill and IUD—act as an abortifacient to the newly created human being. In other words, contraceptive drugs destroy newly created human life in its zygote stage.

The manufacturers of hormonal contraceptives write in their product monographs that if their product does not prevent ovulation, and if it does not sufficiently thicken the cervical mucus to prevent sperm from reaching the ovum, then it ultimately changes the woman's uterine wall to prevent implantation of a newly conceived human life.

Experts call the death toll from hormonal contraceptives "staggering."

Dr. Bogomir Kuhar, a clinical and consultant pharmacist, estimated in 1996 that the total number of newly created human beings destroyed in the U.S. annually since 1973 by the use of oral contraceptives (the pill), contraceptive injections (Depo-Provera), contraceptive implants under the skin (Norplant), contraceptive devices inserted in the reproductive organs (IUD), ranged conservatively between 6.5 million and 11.6 million. Averaging this number and multiplying by the number of years between 1973 and now, a mind-boggling 363.6 million newly created human beings have been aborted through the use of contraceptive drugs.

Compared to the estimated 55 million abortions legally committed in the U.S. in the same time period, contraceptive drugs cause the destruction of more than 6 times the number of human beings.

Professor Charles Rice, professor emeritus at the University of Notre Dame Law School, called contraception the "defining evil of our time," adding that its legitimization has inevitably led to abortion and a host of other evils.

In the final analysis, the strategy of promoting more contraceptive use to decrease abortion approaches the textbook definition of insanity: doing the same thing over and over again and expecting different results. As research suggests, increasing contraception use to decrease abortion is like trying to extinguish a roaring conflagration with a liquid called gasoline.

The real solution is suggested by the correspondent in Doughart's piece, namely a "retooling of people's minds." Young people need to be educated about responsible sexual behavior. They must be educated to see marriage as the only appropriate context for sexual activity and that such activity is ordered to the union of the spouses and to the procreation of children.

The notion of 'accidental pregnancy' that has been repeatedly pummeled into the minds of contraceptive users must be replaced by the notion that human life is a gift and that every person has something unique and unrepeatable to bring into the world.

Only a titanic shift in the predominantly promiscuous and amoral attitudes and behaviors that characterize Western society's understanding of sex will end the genocide of innocent human beings through abortion. Such a shift will not gain traction until contraception is recognized as a deadly cancer in human relationships and labeled as a great destroyer of peace. Anyone who is, as Doughart says, "genuinely interested in reducing abortion," should not be afraid to trace a problem to its cause so as to find and implement a real and lasting solution.

"While the presence of estrogenic compounds in our environment has garnered attention, this review has found the contribution of [oral contraceptives] to overall estrogenicity in water is relatively small compared to other natural and synthetic estrogens."

Birth Control Poses Minimal Environmental Risk

Amber Wise, Kacie O'Brien, and Tracey Woodruff

In the following viewpoint, Amber Wise, Kacie O'Brien, and Tracey Woodruff argue that the use of oral contraceptives does not significantly contribute to environmental pollution caused by the leaching of various chemicals into the water supply. Specifically, they contend that birth control is only one small part of a larger environmental problem related to the leaching of chemicals into the water supply and should not be unjustly targeted in this matter for political reasons. Wise, O'Brien, and Woodruff are researchers with the Program on Reproductive Health and the Environment at the University of California, San Francisco.

As you read, consider the following questions:

1. According to the authors, from where are the estrogenic compounds polluting the environment coming?

2. What three pesticides mentioned in the viewpoint have estrogenic or antiandrogenic properties?

3. According to the authors, why should we not place too much of the blame for estrogenic compound pollution on birth control?

Recent observed feminization of aquatic animals has raised concerns about estrogenic compounds in water supplies and the potential for these chemicals to reach drinking water. Public perception frequently attributes this feminization to oral contraceptives (OCs) in wastewater and raises concerns that exposure to OCs in drinking water may contribute to the recent rise in human reproductive problems. This [viewpoint] reviews the literature regarding various sources of estrogens, in surface, source and drinking water, with an emphasis on the active molecule that comes from OCs. It includes discussion of the various agricultural, industrial, and municipal sources and outlines the contributions of estrogenic chemicals to the estrogenicity of waterways and estimates that the risk of exposure to synthetic estrogens in drinking water on human health is negligible. This [viewpoint] also provides recommendations for strategies to better understand all the potential sources of estrogenic compounds in the environment and possibilities to reduce the levels of estrogenic chemicals in the water supply.

Introduction

The recent increase in examples of intersex fish and organisms found in global waterways has led people to be concerned about estrogenic compounds in the environment. Often, oral contraceptives (OCs) are blamed, as they are an easily identifiable source of estrogen, with 11.6 million women of reproductive age using OCs in the U.S. Use of OCs allows women a significant level of reproductive freedom and additionally has societal and global ramifications on population levels. However, after wastewater treatment, low levels of the main estrogenic ingredient in OCs, 17α-ethinyl estradiol (EE2), have been detected in some surface waters, and this has caused some concern about drinking water contamination. The Endocrine Society recently published a position statement expressing concern that low level, chronic exposure to such environmental endocrine disruptors cause or contribute to adverse human health effects. Intersex fish have been observed near sewage treatment plants in the U.S., across Europe, and in Japan. There is growing concern that a connection exists between estrogenic surface water, the occurrence of intersex fish in these rivers, lakes, and streams, and the rise in human reproductive problems. The peer-reviewed literature and popular media have pointed to EE2 from OCs as a major estrogenic endocrine disrupting chemical contributing to these phenomena. We review the scientific literature to qualitatively assess the contribution of other estrogenic chemicals to the estrogenicity of waterways, to evaluate the pathway of EE2 from ingestion to drinking water, and to explore what is known about the effects of EE2 exposure in drinking water on human health. Studies from Western Europe and the U.S. are highlighted because they have similar industrial practices and contraceptive use. We conclude with possible solutions to reducing the presence of estrogenic compounds, including EE2, in water.

Sources of Estrogens and Estrogenic Compounds. Many chemicals found in our waterways, both natural and synthetic, have the ability to mimic or disrupt the natural estrogens found in humans and animals. Estrogenic chemicals of varying potency and persistence originate from agriculture, industry, humans, household products, and other pharmaceuticals. . . .

Background on Human Estrogens and OCs. The human body has three naturally occurring steroid estrogens: estrone (E1), 17-β estradiol (E2), and estriol (E3), with the synthetic estrogen EE2's structure being most similar to that of E2. The potency of these estrogens are typically measured in relation to E2 (having a value of 1) and are estimated to have the following relative potencies: EE2: 2.0; E2: 1; E1: 0.2–0.4; E3: 0.024–0.026. These values have been determined by estrogen receptor binding *in vitro* assays or vitellogenin induction in male juvenile fish. It is important to note that *in vitro* responses have been known to underestimate *in vivo* responses from more complex wastewater, and potencies can vary somewhat depending on the determination method.

While there are many different versions of oral contraceptives, most OCs are a combination of an estrogen and a progestin, and the most widely used synthetic estrogen is 17α-ethinyl estradiol (EE2) with an average daily dose of 30–35 μg of EE2 per pill. The progestin in combination pills is typically present in higher concentrations (≥ 1 mg per pill).

Human Sources. Human urine is often cited as the main source of natural and synthetic estrogens in the aquatic environment. Humans excrete the natural estrogens E1, E2, and E3. . . . In addition, several synthetic estrogens, ingested through pharmaceuticals, can be also be excreted and enter wastewater. The Dutch Central Bureau of Statistics evaluated the proportion of estrogen excretion, including EE2 by different groups based on the total population figures of 2001 and estimated that EE2 accounts for approximately 1% of the total human excretion of estrogens in the Netherlands. In 2001, 43% of Dutch females of reproductive age used OCs, compared to 28% in the U.S. Therefore, the excretion of EE2 as a fraction of total estrogens in the U.S. is likely less than 1%.

Natural estrogens are also used in other prescribed drugs. We identified one study that provides estimates of the contribution of natural endogenous estrogens (E1, E2, E3), prescription form estrogens (E1, E2, E3), and prescribed synthetic estrogen (EE2) to drinking water estrogen levels. The estimates are derived from the Pharmaceutical Assessment and Transport Evaluation (PhATE) model. . . . PhATE modeling integrates data from source emissions and migration in the environment to model and predict environmental concentrations of chemicals. EE2 has the lowest predicted environmental concentration in U.S. drinking water compared to natural estrogens in the human diet (such as from intake of dairy or soy), and is generally lower than naturally produced and prescription endogenous estrogens. It is still lower than E2 after considering relative potency.

Other estrogenic pharmaceutical drugs are excreted by users and can contribute to the estrogenicity of waterways. Of these are two highly prescribed pharmaceuticals, hormone replacement therapy (HRT) (the main active component is conjugated equine estrogens) and veterinary medicine pharmaceuticals, with greater usage in the U.S. in 1995 compared to EE2. . . . Even though the number of women who take HRT has declined since 2002, the current values are estimated to be similar to 1998 levels. In the United States, between 10% and 25% of women between the ages of 50 and 79 are currently using HRT and an estimated 28% of reproductive-age women use OCs. A report by [L.D.] Arcand-Hoy estimates both HRT and veterinary medicine pharmaceuticals represent more prescribed estrogens per year than OCs. We identified only one study from the UK [United Kingdom] in 2009 which evaluated the environmental impact of conjugated equine estrogens (CEEs) from HRT in four sewage treatment systems. Equine estrogens and their metabolites were present in all sewage influent samples, and 83% of the effluent samples had concentrations similar to EE2 (0.07–2.6 ng/L). The CEEs were taken up by effluent-exposed fish and induced estrogenic responses including hepatic growth and the production of the egg-yolk precursor protein, vitellogenin, at concentrations as low as

0.6–4.2 ng/L, and the potencies of these estrogens were found to be 2.4–3490% greater than the potency of E2. This study provides evidence that estrogens from HRT are discharged at measurable levels which can influence fish health into the aquatic environment.

Ingestion, Metabolism, and Excretion of EE2. . . . EE2 primarily enters the water treatment system as domestic sewage via excretion by women prescribed OCs. It is estimated women on OCs fully metabolize 20–48% of the daily dose of EE2. The rest of the daily dose is excreted in either its original form or as EE2 sulfate or glucuronide conjugates. . . . About 60% of the ingested EE2 is excreted in urine or feces, primarily in the conjugated form, where most of it is deconjugated back to EE2 in the environment. It is assumed that EE2 glucuronides deconjugate to the original form in sewage treatment plants, water, or the environment.

Fate and Transport After Excretion. Levels of natural steroid estrogens and EE2 are higher in sewage influents than effluents, evidence that sewage treatment plants remove a portion of the synthetic hormone. The average concentration of EE2 in both influent and effluent is also less than the natural steroid estrogens, E1 and E2.

Activated sludge and other effective methods of sewage treatment are sufficient in removing most estrogenic compounds, as shown by comparison of sewage influents and effluents. The efficacy of estrogen removal during sewage treatment depends on the specific process and conditions, with several wastewater treatment plants able to remove EE2 at ≥80–98% efficiency. Activated sludge has repeatedly been shown to remove estrogenic compounds consistently removing over 85% of EE2 and E2. EE2 was also reported to be degraded completely by nitrifying activated sludge in six days, converting EE2 into hydrophilic compounds. Moreover, studies show that treatment of water with chlorine removes between 80–95% of EE2, and treatment with ozone removes 95–99% of EE2.

Surface Water Studies. EE2 and other natural estrogens can enter surface water through wastewater treatment effluent and runoff from agricultural sources. Monitoring studies of surface water use a variety of EE2 detection methods to find a range of values for EE2 and natural human and animal steroid estrogens.... In general, in studies where steroid hormones were detected above the detection limit, EE2 is detected with the lowest frequency and at the lowest concentration in comparison to E2 and E1. Studies reviewed by the Environment Agency of the UK indicated that when EE2 was detected in surface waters it was generally found at concentrations less than 5 ng/L and often below 1 ng/L.

A 1999 US Geological Survey (USGS) of 139 U.S. streams identified as high risk for domestic and industrial pollution found EE2 was measured in 5.7% of these high risk regions (limit of detection = 5 ng/L). While this limit of detection is somewhat higher than other studies, the relatively low occurrence of EE2 detection is consistent with those of previously published investigations that have lower limits of detection.

Drinking Water Studies. Monitoring Studies. There are a small number of reports that measure levels of EE2 in drinking water. The studies that report estrogen levels in source and finished drinking water ... primarily find that EE2 is below the limit of detection (LOD = 0.05 ng/L-1 ng/L) in drinking water in the UK and the U.S. With the exception of one study in Germany, the UK Environment Agency concluded from data available through 2004 that EE2 and natural steroid estrogens were not detected in drinking water above the LOD of 0.3 ng/L in a review of all available studies from Europe, the U.S., and Japan.

Studies that measure EE2 in drinking water in the U.S. suggest when present, it is typically at levels lower than the detection level used by the USGS (1 ng/L).

Model Estimates. A study published in early 2009 using PhATE to estimate EE2 levels in U.S. found that EE2 sewage effluent levels would range from 0.4 ng/L to 13 ng/L. The 13 ng/L is an upper estimate assuming no metabolism in the body and no removal by sewage treatment plants. The lower estimate of 0.4 ng/L assumes 50% metabolism and 82% removal by sewage treatment removal. EE2 concentrations in surface waters would be reduced further by in-stream dilution and degradation. The estimates also do not account for drinking water treatment. Treatment methods for drinking water vary in their effectiveness to remove estrogens, but a study by [M.J.] Benotti (2009) reports removal rates of 80–99% for EE2, E1, and E2 via chlorine or ozone oxidation. Thus, the PhATE model predicts less than 1 ng/L of EE2 in drinking water. This model is useful in identifying measurement outliers and suggests measurements greater than 1 ng/L may come from locally generated sources (e.g., downstream of a pharmaceutical manufacturing facility or agricultural waste stream) or that further evaluation of measurements is warranted to ensure accuracy.

Agricultural Sources. Livestock excrete the same natural estrogens (E1, E2, and E3) as humans, and there is a growing body of research showing elevated estrogen levels in surface and groundwater downstream of farms and agricultural land. In the U.S., livestock produce 133 million tons of manure per year; 13-fold more solid waste than human sanitary waste production. . . . An important source of agricultural effluents is from concentrated animal [feeding] operations (CAFOs). The effluents are untreated, and their use as an agricultural fertilizer is growing. In addition to spreading manure for fertilizer, livestock waste can enter the environment when rain causes overflow, or from runoff and leaching into the soils near manure storage facilities. In addition to naturally excreted hormones, livestock are also given prescribed hormones. However, it is difficult to determine the contribution of natural versus pharmaceutical estrogen to total livestock estrogen excretion, as we found little information to distinguish the two. One study in 1995 found the use of veterinary estrogens was more than five times the use of OCs. . . . In human raw sewage effluents, E2 varies between 0.5 and 125 ng/L, while animal waste contains levels of E2 ranging from 30–2500 ng/L.

A number of studies in Europe and the U.S. have measured or estimated the contribution of livestock to total estrogens in water. In the UK, it has been estimated that if just 1% of the estrogens excreted by livestock reached water sources, this would account for 15% of all the estrogens in water. Another study estimates that animal waste contributes 90% of total estrogens in the environment. E2 concentrations were found to be as high as 3500 ng/L in surface runoff from grasslands in Arkansas where poultry litter was applied as fertilizer. U.S. aquifers under areas covered in animal manure were found to have an E2 concentration of 37.6 ng/L, and groundwater measurements of E2 ranged from 6 to 66 ng/L in five springs in northwest Arkansas where poultry litter and cattle manure were applied.

A study of 113 surface and groundwater samples in northern California found that only 5% contained concentrations of estrogenic compounds high enough to induce a vitellogenin response using an mRNA detection screen in juvenile rainbow trout. They determined that the few samples that induced vitellogenin response were from agricultural-dominated waterways.

The agricultural studies indicate that livestock effluents and runoff from manure are likely to be a significant source of natural estrogens in the waterways and have the potential to reach drinking water.

Pesticides. Many pesticides are known to have estrogenic or antiandrogenic properties in a variety of species. Some of them include the widely used atrazine, vinclozolin, and organochlorine pesticides, such as DDT [dichlorodiphenyltrichloroethane]. Because of widespread agricultural use, these pesticides have been detected in surface water, groundwater, and drinking water at varying levels. Atrazine is especially mobile in the environment and is known to precipitate in rainfall. Pesticides are present in streams in 97% of agricultural and urban areas, often at levels above quality benchmark doses and often more than one pesticide is present in any one location. In a USGS survey of U.S. drinking water wells, 70% of the samples contained at least one volatile organic compound, pesticide, or anthropogenic nitrate, with values ranging from 100 ng/L-100 µg/L. While the relative potencies of these pesticides are typically 100–1000 times less than E2, detected values are often 10–10,000 times higher than natural estrogens and adverse effects can be seen on aquatic amphibians at levels as low as 0.1 ppb and at ppm levels for other wildlife. While it is beyond the scope of this [viewpoint] to include an in-depth discussion of the estrogenic contributions of pesticides, it is clear the widespread detection and, in some areas, high levels of detection are cause for concern.

Plant-Based Sources. Phytoestrogens (estrogens produced by plants) are found in various plant matter, such as nuts and legumes, and can be excreted by humans and livestock after eating. They are also present in high quantities near soy-processing facilities and other plant-based industries such as biodiesel plants. Their potency varies, with values ranging from 10^4–10^5 times less potent than E2. Phytoestrogen entry into the environment is not as well studied, and they are largely ignored as a potential contributor to the estrogenicity of water. Yet, a recent study of 19 industrial wastewater streams in Minnesota and Iowa found plant estrogens at levels 250 times higher than the amount needed to cause feminization in fish. The elevated levels of these phytoestrogens were attributed to nearby industrial facilities including soy milk factories, biodiesel factories, and dairies. This study also measured elevated phytoestrogen levels downstream from wastewater treatment plants. While standard treatment can remove more

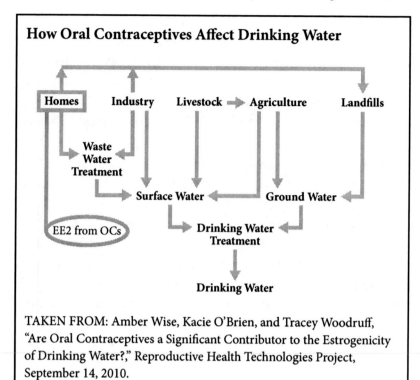

How Oral Contraceptives Affect Drinking Water

TAKEN FROM: Amber Wise, Kacie O'Brien, and Tracey Woodruff, "Are Oral Contraceptives a Significant Contributor to the Estrogenicity of Drinking Water?," Reproductive Health Technologies Project, September 14, 2010.

than 90% of the phytoestrogens, industrial factories that process large amounts of soy, plant matter for biodiesel, and dairy products are often found in small towns which may not have the municipal treatment capabilities to remove phytoestrogens from the water. Thus, in certain locations, plant-based phytoestrogens may be an important contributor to the estrogenicity of the water.

Industrial Chemicals. Industrial chemicals can enter waterways through a variety of means, including point-sources like manufacturing facilities, domestic and industrial wastewater effluents, runoff from urban areas, and leaching from landfills. There is a great deal of uncertainty regarding the number of industrial chemicals with estrogenic activity since many chemicals are untested for this effect. There are many industrial chemicals present in the environment known to have estrogenic properties of varying potencies, including bisphenol A [BPA], polychlorinated biphenyls, brominated flame retardants, alkylphenols, and others. One study of several classes of phenolic compounds found levels of octylphenol, nonylphenol, BPA, and other phenolic compounds from 0.13–3.6 µg/L in untreated wastewater and 0.16–0.36 µg/L in treated wastewater.

When studying estrogenicity of water samples, often a "total estrogenicity" is measured in addition to the concentrations of E1, E2, and less often, EE2. "Total estrogenicity" is usually determined in E2 equivalents by measuring *in vitro* binding to estrogen receptors. However, several studies measuring the total estrogenicity of wastewater report that samples contained more estrogenic activity than was predicted from the chemical analysis of E1, E2, and EE2 concentrations, indicating other contributing factors. Another study that investigated feminization of fish concludes that xenoestrogens and (as yet unknown) chemicals with antiandrogenic properties also contribute to sexual disruption of aquatic species.

One specific example of industrial chemicals with the ability to disrupt the estrogenic hormone system is the alkylphenols. U.S. production of alkylphenol ethoxylates exceeds 500 million pounds per year, with nonylphenol's production alone estimated at 340 million pounds. The alkylphenols are used primarily for cleaning and sanitizing agents. The nonylphenol and octylphenol molecules, and their degradation products can independently induce vitellogenin production and inhibit testicular growth in fish at levels as low as 10 µg/L. Nonylphenol caused adverse reproductive effects in medaka fish at levels as low as 17.7 µg/L, and octylphenol significantly increased vitellogenin production at levels as low as 3 µg/L.

The US Geological Survey reported that nonylphenol was one of the most frequently detected industrial chemicals in surface waters with a median concentration of 0.8 µg/L. It is estimated 60% of the alkyphenols produced end up in the aquatic environment after sewage treatment, either the original molecule, or as shorter chain alkyl degradation products. Effluents from domestic sewage treatment plants can contain the original alkylphenolic compounds at concentrations greater than 100 μg/L, and industrial effluents can contain significantly more. Additionally, other chemicals which can effect estrogenic activity, such as BPA or triclosan, have been found at 25 ng/L and 1.2 ng/L, respectively, in U.S. drinking water.

Alkylphenols are one example of the potentially thousands of chemicals used in industry with the ability to disrupt the estrogenic hormone system and also have the ability to contribute to the estrogenic activity in water.

Public Health Implications. It has been suggested that environmental exposure to estrogenic chemicals are a risk factor for several human health outcomes including . . . testicular cancer, breast cancer, endometriosis, and decreased sperm counts. However, uncertainty in the science remains about the nature and magnitude of risks that can occur from low-level exposures to estrogenic chemicals. The Endocrine Society has published a position statement stating "evidence for adverse reproductive outcomes (infertility, cancers, malformations) from exposure to endocrine disrupting chemicals [EDCs] is strong, and there is mounting evidence for effects on . . . thyroid, neuroendocrine, obesity and metabolism, and insulin and glucose homeostasis." The statement details the many EDCs, both estrogenic and those disrupting other hormones, which have shown adverse health effects in animal models. An additional concern with EDCs and other chemical exposures is that it cannot be assumed that there is a threshold for adverse health effects especially for vulnerable populations, which has also been echoed by the National Academy of Sciences.

A study published in early 2010, using the PhATE model, estimated exposure levels of natural and synthetic estrogens from drinking water and compared drinking water exposure to exposure from both milk intake for children and dietary intake for adults. The study used the upper estimate of the PhATE model of EE2 in drinking water and predicted that exposure to EE2 in drinking water is at most 82 times lower than background dietary exposure to estrogens for adults. The study estimated that a child's exposure to estrogens from drinking water was about 150–250-fold smaller than their exposure to estrogens from drinking milk. All comparisons of estrogenicity were made using E2 equivalents and thus accounts for the stronger potency of EE2.

Discussion

While the overall contribution of EE2 to drinking water estrogenicity appears to be less than from other sources, EE2 is an additional endocrine disrupting chemical that could contribute to the feminization of aquatic species. Thus, there are still steps that could to be taken to reduce levels of EE2 and begin to address the larger issue of endocrine disrupting chemicals in our environment.

Improved Wastewater Treatment. EE2 possesses the potential to adversely influence wildlife if local concentrations exceed levels of concern. Wastewater treatment and drinking water treatment vary in their abilities to remove EE2 and offer a point of intervention to reduce the levels of EE2 reaching animals and humans. While there is a range of effectiveness, many existing sewage treatment plants have been found to dramatically reduce EE2 concentrations in the influent. Updating to more effective methods and standardizing sewage treatment plants could contribute to reducing levels of EE2 and other estrogenic contaminants.

Improved Detection Methods and Monitoring Programs. Inexpensive, standardized methods for detection and determining concentrations of estrogenicity should be developed for use by city and state water departments to understand the extent of the issue. . . . Until a more sensitive analysis of effluents, surface water, and drinking water is performed in the

U.S., it is not possible to know the true distribution of EE2 in our water supplies. Local water departments already test their water regularly to monitor for contaminants. The addition of a centralized, nationwide reporting mechanism for reporting levels of a spectrum of the most prevalent and/or biological significant estrogenic contaminants (including EE2) would improve the ability to assess potential risks and the identification of at-risk regions. Standardized methods for detection will help ensure adequate removal of contaminants. Until there is routine screening for EE2 and other estrogenic compounds with appropriate limits of detection, it will be hard to fully characterize the contributors to the estrogenicity of U.S. waterways.

Improved Estrogenicity Tests. Estrogenicity tests give varying results on the estrogenicity of a compound. *In vitro* methods vary in their measurements of estrogenicity from each other and vary greatly from *in vivo* methods. Many *in vitro* methods only measure binding affinity to the estrogen receptor which does not account for the many possible biological pathways through which an endocrine disruptor may act. Improved testing assays and standards for measuring potency would improve the ability to compare results across studies. The EPA [Environmental Protection Agency] started an endocrine disrupting chemicals screening program in 1996 but has not screened any chemicals to date and has only recently released a list of EDCs for which to screen.

Chemical Policy Reform. There are tens of thousands of chemicals (US-EPA) for which we have little or no data on their potential to negatively influence health. Additionally, current regulatory structure has been identified as insufficient to require the necessary testing and subsequent regulation of harmful chemicals. Moreover, previous programs enacted by Congress to develop and implement testing protocols to identify endocrine disrupting chemicals have been inadequate due to significant delays in implementation and concerns about the sufficiency of testing. Requiring information on the potential toxicity for chemicals on the market is one critical step in identifying and reducing harmful chemical exposures. Efforts are underway to address this legislative gap with recent introductions of new legislation in Congress. New legislation and regulatory activities need to address both required testing and ensure that estrogenicity, as part of endocrine disruption, be adequately addressed in testing and implementation protocol.

Reducing Overall Use of EE2. Even though the limited evidence indicates EE2 is a relatively small contributor to the overall estrogenicity of drinking water, efforts to reduce the source of EE2, as part of an overall strategy for reducing sources of other estrogenic substances in general, should be pursued. These include low-dose OCs, which may reduce EE2 excretion by 28.5–43%, or reformulation to increase the efficacy of absorption and lower excretion. Additionally, there are nonhormonal methods of contraception including the copper intrauterine device (IUD), diaphragms, or condoms.

Further Research. There are many areas of research which would contribute to a better understanding of the risk of EE2 and other estrogenic compounds to the public's health. These research areas include the following:

- Investigating the role of agricultural sources such as CAFOs and fertilizer applications to the overall estrogenicity of surface, ground, and drinking water. Further efforts are need to identify effective intervention strategies, including policy approaches to reduce contribution to water contamination.

- Combined effects or additivity of endocrine disruptors should be accounted for to better characterize the threat posed by the combination and mixtures of the variety of chemicals found in surface and drinking water.

- Toxicological assessments of common estrogenic contaminants and mixtures should be done, especially the xenoestrogens like nonylphenols found in surface waters.

Conclusion

While the presence of estrogenic compounds in our environment has garnered attention, this review has found the contribution of OCs to overall estrogenicity in water is relatively small compared to other natural and synthetic estrogens. The risk of EE2 in surface waters to wildlife health may pose problems locally, but the risk to human health posed by EE2 at levels in drinking water appears to be minimal. However, more research is needed to understand how EE2 combines with the many other estrogenic sources to affect wildlife and human health. Removing EE2 from the market will have a negligible effect on the environment, aquatic life, and human health. However, removing OCs from the market would be detrimental to women's health and their ability to decide the timing and spacing of their children and would have societal and global implications. Future efforts to reduce the overall estrogenicity of water should take a broad approach to reducing the contribution from the multiple sources, particularly those that are unregulated or that are untreated.

> "Reducing population growth and lowering fertility will improve communities' resilience and adaptive capacity in the short term, as well as reduce greenhouse gas emissions. In the long term, population reductions could reduce the risk of climate impacts."

Birth Control Could Help the Environment, but Not Quickly

Niina Heikkinen

In the following viewpoint, Niina Heikkinen argues that birth control is needed to avoid the potentially disastrous environmental consequences of overpopulation. Asserting that the world's population is growing out of control and quickly using up all of the planet's natural resources, Heikkinen says it is imperative that individuals recognize the importance of family planning and birth control before it is too late. Heikkinen is a reporter for E&E Publishing's ClimateWire.

As you read, consider the following questions:

1. According to Heikkinen, the global population is expected to grow by what numbers by 2050 and 2100, respectively?

2. According to Heikkinen, how would making birth control more widely available affect the emission of greenhouse gases?

3. How long would it take to halve the world's population, according to the viewpoint?

This week [in October 2014], a group of researchers promoted a different kind of global approach to addressing climate change: voluntary family planning.

Though their proposal may raise eyebrows, researchers at the Population Reference Bureau and Worldwatch Institute say what they are advocating will both empower women and preserve the environment. They recently formed a joint working group of health, climate and population experts from around the world. They are drafting a report on how family planning could be incorporated into governments' environmental policy.

Family Planning as a Component of Environmental Policy

With an estimated global population of over 7.2 billion people, there is increasing concern that finite natural resources will no longer be able to keep up with increasing demands. According to a 2013 U.N. [United Nations] report, the global population is expected to grow to 9.6 billion by 2050 and 10.9 billion by 2100.

Reducing population growth and lowering fertility will improve communities' resilience and adaptive capacity in the short term, as well as reduce greenhouse gas emissions. In the long term, population reductions could reduce the risk of climate impacts, according to the working group. It presented its proposals at a forum at the Woodrow Wilson International Center for Scholars in Washington, D.C., yesterday.

"Far too often in the past, it has been approached as giving up freedom, rather than looking at family planning as creating greater freedom and greater happiness," said Alexander Ochs, director of the climate and energy program at the Worldwatch Institute.

He described the working group's promotion of family planning as a "women-centered rights-based approach" that focused on the "urgency and right of determining the timing and spacing of having children."

Efforts to control fertility improve maternal and child health and welfare, while also conserving natural resources, he added.

"This is not a new connection that we're making; even in Washington, these things are being discussed," said Jason Bremner, the associate vice president and program director of the population, health and environment program at the Population Reference Bureau. "Yet family planning benefits for climate change have not trickled into policy."

The speakers at the forum said that while the concept of governments implementing voluntary population control measures used to be more controversial, more countries are recognizing that growing populations are putting a strain on natural resources, food security and human health.

Gaps in Implementation, Funding

In its latest report, the Intergovernmental Panel on Climate Change (IPCC) included a section on the relationship between family planning and climate, stating that a growing global population is one cause of increased greenhouse gas emissions. The report cited a study estimating a 30 percent decrease in emissions by 2100 if women without access to birth control were provided with contraceptives.

In particular, the IPCC identified the Sahel region of Africa as being especially in need of family planning efforts because of a combination of high fertility and high vulnerability to climate change in the area.

"This is important not only in poor countries, however, but also some rich ones like the USA, where there is unmet need for reproductive health services as well as high CO_2 emissions per capita," the 2014 report said.

Other countries are also recognizing the need for family planning. Among the 39 U.N. National Adaptation Programmes of Action, which identify priorities for adapting to climate change in the poorest nations, 37 connected population growth to climate change.

Six recognized family planning or reproductive health as a component of an adaptation strategy. But only two had actual projects in place, according to a presentation by Karen Hardee, a senior associate and Evidence Project director at the Population Council.

Still, lack of funding remains a barrier to project development, said Clive Mutunga, a family planning and environment technical adviser for the U.S. Agency for International Development.

"Now trying to link the policies into the programs is the challenge. We need to move forward to specific programs to implement on the ground," he said at the forum.

Soaring Growth vs. Ominous Climate Impacts

Even if family planning is widely adopted across the globe, a recent study suggests that the effects on climate change will be minimal in the near term.

Researchers at the University of Adelaide in Australia found that even dramatic population reductions would not be enough to have much of an environmental effect for most of the 21st century.

They published their findings in the journal *Proceedings of the National Academy of Sciences* on Tuesday.

Using scenario-based matrix modeling, the researchers tested what the global population would look like after a hy-

Birth Control and Population

If measures are taken now, we could still keep the 2050 world population at around 8 billion. We have to ensure that the population can be slowed by purely voluntary means and within a human rights framework. We need to galvanize the political will to make it happen and invest now so that family planning options are universally available. Fail to do so, and we may give birth to a new, difficult era of poverty instead.

Malcolm Potts and Martha Campbell, "Foreign Policy: Without Birth Control, Planet Doomed," NPR, May 11, 2011.

pothetical catastrophe killed 2 billion people over a five-year period around 2060. They found that the population by the end of the century would still reach 8.5 billion by 2100.

A second scenario in which 6 billion people were killed around 2040 would result in a population of 5.1 billion in 2100.

The researchers wrote, "Even if the human collective were to pull as hard as possible on the total fertility policy lever (via a range of economic, medical and social interventions) the result would be ineffective in mitigating the immediately looming global sustainability crises (including anthropogenic climate disruption), for which we need to have major solutions well under way by 2050 and essentially solved by 2100."

"I hope this is taken as a wake-up call and a sobering reminder of how long we've neglected the population issue," said the study's lead author, Corey Bradshaw.

The computer modeling was not meant to predict what the population is likely to be in coming decades, but rather to see how quickly the population size could respond to likely and unlikely scenarios, according to Bradshaw, the director of ecological modeling at the University of Adelaide.

Long Lead Times for Solutions

He pointed out that population growth has been so dramatic in recent decades that roughly 14 percent of the humans who have ever lived are alive today. At the same time, people are consuming more per capita than ever before in the world's most affluent nations.

The researchers predicted that it would take about 100 years to halve the population and perhaps many more years after that to reverse the environmental impacts. "We don't have that much time; we have decades," he said.

A more immediately effective approach that could reduce environmental harm would be policies and initiatives focused on curtailing the consumption of natural resources, according to the researchers.

That is not to suggest that family planning is not an important strategy. If, for instance, the world adopted a policy of one child per woman by 2045, that would reduce the population by 3 billion.

More realistic measures could also produce tangible population reductions.

"If you could work slightly towards reducing unwanted pregnancies, that could be hundreds of millions of fewer people born," Bradshaw said.

Taken a step further, if the worldwide average fertility could be down to two children per woman by 2020, rather than the current 2.37 average, that would result in 777 million fewer people by 2050.

"That's nothing to sneeze at," he said.

Periodical and Internet Sources Bibliography

The following articles have been selected to supplement the diverse views presented in this chapter.

Brian Clowes	"Culture of Life 101 . . . 'What Are the Environmental Impacts of Hormonal Birth Control?," *The Wanderer*, March 10, 2015.
Michael Brendan Dougherty and Pascal-Emmanuel Gobry	"Time to Admit It: The Church Has Always Been Right on Birth Control," Business Insider, February 8, 2012.
Darryl Fears	"Fish Don't Want Birth Control, but Scientists Say They Get It from Your Pill," *Washington Post*, March 30, 2015.
Laurie Goering	"Experts Say Birth Control Access Key to Curbing Climate Change," *World Post*, February 3, 2015.
Katherine Harmon	"Free Birth Control Access Can Reduce Abortion Rate by More than Half," *Scientific American*, October 4, 2012.
Abby Johnson	"Sorry Folks. Contraception Access Increases Abortions. And Here's the Proof," LifeSiteNews.com, March 11, 2015.
Amanda Marcotte	"Abortion Rate Hits Record Low. Thanks, Birth Control Advocates!," *Slate*, February 3, 2014.
Wynne Parry	"Water Pollution Caused by Birth Control Poses Dilemma," LiveScience, May 23, 2012.
Jason Plautz	"The Climate-Change Solution No One Will Talk About," *Atlantic*, November 1, 2014.
John Seager	"Birth Control and the Human-Wildlife Connection," *Huffington Post*, May 1, 2015.

For Further Discussion

Chapter 1

1. Maria Pawlowska argues that access to birth control should be considered a human right. She says that a woman's "right to contraceptive information and services is, in fact, an element of a number of key basic human rights." Name these rights Pawlowska mentions and state whether you or disagree with her argument. Explain your reasoning.

2. Kimberly Leonard argues that teenagers should have easier access to intrauterine devices (IUDs). Do you agree with her argument? Why, or why not?

3. Zoe Zorka argues that a male birth control shot would be broadly beneficial, while Kaitlin Reilly contends that male contraception could potentially be disempowering for women. With which author do you agree more? Explain your reasoning.

Chapter 2

1. Alissa Light argues that employers should be required to cover the cost of birth control for their employees. Do you think she makes a valid point? Do you find any faults with her argument? Explain.

2. Jack Kenny and Jonathan D. Sarna take different stances as to the constitutionality of the Patient Protection and Affordable Care Act's birth control mandate. After reading both viewpoints, do you think the birth control mandate is constitutional? Explain your reasoning.

3. Andrew Koppelman and Ian Millhiser express opposing views on the wisdom of the Supreme Court's decision in *Burwell v. Hobby Lobby Stores*. In your opinion, which author makes a stronger argument? Explain.

Chapter 3

1. Amanda Marcotte argues that birth control should be available over the counter. Do you agree with her? Why, or why not?

2. Virginia Sole-Smith and Jessica Kiley espouse different opinions on concerns about the potential health risks associated with the birth control pill. Do you think taking the birth control pill is worth the risk? Why, or why not? Explain, citing text from the viewpoints to support your answer.

3. Mathew Lu argues that emergency contraception is effectively a form of abortion. What evidence does he put forth to support this claim? Do you think his reasoning is correct? Why, or why not?

Chapter 4

1. Peter Baklinski argues that the use of birth control increases the abortion rate rather than lowers it. Do you agree with his argument? Why, or why not?

2. How do Amber Wise, Kacie O'Brien, and Tracey Woodruff confront the notion that birth control is significantly harmful to the environment? Do you think they make a compelling argument? Why, or why not?

3. Niina Heikkinen argues that contraception is important as a means of population control. She particularly mentions population growth's effect on climate change. How do you think birth control can impact climate change? Explain, citing text from the viewpoint to support your answer.

Organizations to Contact

The editors have compiled the following list of organizations concerned with the issues debated in this book. The descriptions are derived from materials provided by the organizations. All have publications or information available for interested readers. The list was compiled on the date of publication of the present volume; the information provided here may change. Be aware that many organizations take several weeks or longer to respond to inquiries, so allow as much time as possible.

Advocates for Youth
2000 M Street NW, Suite 750, Washington, DC 20036
(202) 419-3420 • fax: (202) 419-1448
website: www.advocatesforyouth.org

Since it was founded as the Center for Population Options in 1980, Advocates for Youth has worked to provide responsible and effective sexual health strategies and information for adolescents in the United States and developing countries around the world. In serving as a reliable and accessible source of information on everything from contraception to teen pregnancy, Advocates for Youth aims to help adolescents make informed, responsible sexual health decisions. Among the organization's diverse array of programs is the Adolescent Contraceptive Access Initiative, which is designed to provide teens with reliable information on birth control and today's many contraceptive options. Through its website, Advocates for Youth makes available a large collection of publications, such as reports, fact sheets, and program assessments.

American Life League (ALL)
PO Box 1350, Stafford, VA 22555
(540) 659-4171 • fax: (540) 659-2586
website: www.all.org

The American Life League (ALL) is a nonprofit pro-life organization dedicated to eradicating what it views as immoral sexual health practices. Among its many initiatives is "The Pill

Kills," a campaign against the birth control pill. Through this campaign, ALL seeks to highlight the pill's inherent dangers, including its potential to cause serious health complications and even death. ALL also decries the pill as harmful to marriages because the pill limits procreation, interferes with spousal relationships, and decreases female libido. On its website, ALL publishes talking points, news, information on its various campaigns and programs, and details on how people can get involved in its fight against the use and sale of oral contraceptives.

Association of Reproductive Health Professionals (ARHP)
1300 Nineteenth Street NW, Suite 200
Washington, DC   20036
(202) 446-3825
e-mail: ARHP@arhp.org
website: www.arhp.org

The Association of Reproductive Health Professionals (ARHP) is a medical association of reproductive health professionals who share an interest in networking and sharing the latest and most relevant information on programs, policies, technology, and breakthroughs in the reproductive health field. ARHP takes an active role in developing evidence-based programs with the aim of helping its members provide their patients with the best care available. The ARHP website offers members and non-members access to accurate information on birth control, sexually transmitted diseases (STDs), and many other reproductive health issues. ARHP's official peer-reviewed journal, *Contraception: An International Reproductive Health Journal*, highlights cutting-edge research and features commentary on current events and topics in sexual and reproductive health.

Bixby Center for Global Reproductive Health
3333 California Street, Suite 335, Box 0744
San Francisco, CA   94143
(415) 476-4911 • fax: (415) 502-8479
website: bixbycenter.ucsf.edu

Created by the University of California, San Francisco, in 1999, the Bixby Center for Global Reproductive Health works to develop strategies for addressing domestic and international health issues. The Bixby Center's stated goals include developing and evaluating new reproductive health technologies related to contraception and reproductive and maternal health; decreasing maternal mortality; providing training for reproductive health practitioners and researchers; analyzing contemporary reproductive health policies and research; and improving adolescent reproductive and sexual health. On its website, the Bixby Center publishes a wide array of reports on contraception and reproductive health as well as relevant fact sheets, books, videos, issue briefs, and other materials.

Center for Reproductive Rights
199 Water Street, New York, NY   10038
(917) 637-3600 • fax: (917) 637-3666
e-mail: info@reprorights.org
website: reproductiverights.org

The Center for Reproductive Rights is a New York–based legal center dedicated to protecting women's reproductive rights and securing access to birth control and family planning services. As part of this commitment, the center argues cases before an array of different national courts, United Nations committees, and various regional human rights organizations. The center also actively seeks to aid policy makers and legislators in their efforts to enact and strengthen comprehensive and effective reproductive legislation. The center's website hosts a wide variety of in-depth reports, press releases, fact sheets, policy briefs, and other information on reproductive law and policy.

International Consortium for Emergency Contraception (ICEC)
45 Broadway, Suite 320, New York, NY   10006
(212) 941-5300
e-mail: info@cecinfo.org
website: www.cecinfo.org

The International Consortium for Emergency Contraception (ICEC) is an association of international family planning organizations that work together to ensure that safe and effective emergency contraception is accessible to women around the world. ICEC's four main advocacy focuses include emergency contraception and adolescents; legal challenges; improving and protecting access to contraception; and providing emergency services to women during times of crisis. Through its website, ICEC puts forth a range of emergency contraception–related publications that include reports, policy briefs, fact sheets, and issue papers.

National Family Planning & Reproductive Health Association (NFPRHA)
1627 K Street NW, 12th Floor, Washington, DC 20006
(202) 293-3114
e-mail: info@nfprha.org
website: www.nationalfamilyplanning.org

The National Family Planning & Reproductive Health Association (NFPRHA) is a member organization that advocates for family planning administrators and providers who work with low-income and uninsured patients. NFPRHA's mission is to provide its members with training and continuing education to ensure that people everywhere have access to high-quality, federally funded reproductive health care. Through its website, NFPRHA publishes press releases, videos, and family planning profiles, which recount the organization's efforts to serve patients in need.

Planned Parenthood Federation of America
1110 Vermont Avenue NW, Suite 300, Washington, DC 20005
(202) 973-4800 • fax: (202) 296-3242
website: www.plannedparenthood.org

Planned Parenthood Federation of America, the US branch of the International Planned Parenthood Federation, is a nonprofit organization that offers reproductive health and family planning services. Operating more than eight hundred health centers across the country, Planned Parenthood provides quality reproductive health care as part of a concerted effort to prevent unintentional pregnancies through birth control and limit the spread of sexually transmitted diseases through screenings and treatment. Planned Parenthood is also dedicated to empowering adolescents by providing them with accurate and practical information on and access to reliable contraception. In addition, Planned Parenthood publishes fact sheets, studies, news stories, and many other materials on its website.

Reproductive Health Access Project (RHAP)

PO Box 21191, New York, NY   10025
(212) 206-5247 • fax: (314) 584-3260
e-mail: info@reproductiveaccess.org
website: www.reproductiveaccess.org

The Reproductive Health Access Project (RHAP) is an organization that seeks to ensure that all women and teens have easy access to birth control and abortion from their family physician regardless of socioeconomic standing. To that end, RHAP sponsors training, mentoring, and advocacy programs to support primary care clinicians and local reproductive health organizations. As part of its efforts, RHAP research reports, fact sheets, news articles, contraceptive user guides, and other materials are available on the organization's website.

US Department of Health and Human Services (HHS)

200 Independence Avenue SW, Washington, DC   20201
(877) 696-6775
website: www.hhs.gov

The US Department of Health and Human Services (HHS) is a government agency tasked with providing essential health services and protecting the health of all American citizens. HHS works in tandem with state and local governments to develop and implement health programs and policies. In relation to contraception, HHS's aim is to ensure that American women have access to a range of safe and reliable birth control options as well as current, accurate information on the contraceptive products they use. Through its website, HHS provides fact sheets on available birth control options and a range of other educational materials.

Bibliography of Books

A.F. Alexander — *Birth Control, Insurance Coverage, and the Religious Right.* Colorado Springs, CO: Blazing Sword Publishing, 2013.

Fritz Allhoff and Mark Hall, eds. — *The Affordable Care Act Decision: Philosophical and Legal Implications.* New York: Routledge, 2014.

Louis Bourgois and Samuel Cauchois, eds. — *Contraceptives: Role of Cultural Attitudes and Practices, Predictors of Use and Levels of Effectiveness.* Hauppauge, NY: Nova Science Publishers, 2014.

Paula Briggs and Gabor Kovacs, eds. — *Contraception: A Casebook from Menarche to Menopause.* New York: Cambridge University Press, 2013.

Clare Debenham — *Birth Control and the Rights of Women: Post-Suffrage Feminism in the Early Twentieth Century.* London: I.B. Tauris, 2013.

Jonathan Eig — *The Birth of the Pill: How Four Crusaders Reinvented Sex and Launched a Revolution.* New York: W.W. Norton & Company, 2014.

Laura Eldridge — *In Our Control: The Complete Guide to Contraceptive Choices for Women.* New York: Seven Stories Press, 2010.

Peter C. Engelman — *A History of the Birth Control Movement in America.* Santa Barbara, CA: Praeger, 2011.

Suzanne Everett   *Handbook of Contraception and Sexual Health*. New York: Routledge, 2014.

Angel M. Foster and L.L. Wynn, eds.   *Emergency Contraception: The Story of a Global Reproductive Health Technology*. New York: Palgrave Macmillan, 2012.

Angela Franks   *Contraception and Catholicism: What the Church Teaches and Why*. Boston, MA: Pauline Books & Media, 2013.

David H. Gans and Ilya Shapiro   *Religious Liberties for Corporations?: Hobby Lobby, the Affordable Care Act, and the Constitution*. New York: Palgrave Macmillan, 2014.

Holly Grigg-Spall   *Sweetening the Pill: Or How We Got Hooked on Hormonal Birth Control*. Alresford, Hants, UK: Zero Books, 2013.

John Guillebaud and Anne MacGregor   *Contraception: Your Questions Answered*. 6th ed. Philadelphia, PA: Elsevier Health Sciences, 2012.

Melissa Haussman   *Reproductive Rights and the State: Getting the Birth Control, RU-486, and Morning-After Pills and the Gardasil Vaccine to the U.S. Market*. Santa Barbara, CA: Praeger, 2013.

Elaine Tyler May   *America and the Pill: A History of Promise, Peril, and Liberation*. New York: Basic Books, 2011.

Manon Parry — *Broadcasting Birth Control: Mass Media and Family Planning.* New Brunswick, NJ: Rutgers University Press, 2013.

Ross Pelton — *The Pill Problem: How to Protect Your Health from the Side Effects of Oral Contraceptives.* Portland, OR: BookBaby, 2013.

Charles E. Rice — *Contraception and Persecution.* South Bend, IN: St. Augustine's Press, 2014.

Chikako Takeshita — *The Global Biopolitics of the IUD: How Science Constructs Contraceptive Users and Women's Bodies.* Cambridge, MA: MIT Press, 2012.

Austin Tallman — *A Protestant Critique of the Contraception Debate.* Springhill, TN: Tallmann Publications, 2013.

Beverly Vincent and Robert Greenberger — *Frequently Asked Questions About Birth Control.* New York: Rosen Publishing Group, 2011.

Eugene Volokh — *Sebelius v. Hobby Lobby: Corporate Rights and Religious Liberties.* Washington, DC: Cato Institute, 2014.

Toni Weschler — *Taking Charge of Your Fertility: The Definitive Guide to Natural Birth Control, Pregnancy Achievement, and Reproductive Health, 20th Anniversary Edition.* New York: William Morrow, 2015.

| Amy Whitaker and Melissa Gilliam, eds. | *Contraception for Adolescent and Young Adult Women.* New York: Springer, 2014. |
| Mimi Zieman, Robert A. Hatcher, and Ariel Z. Allen | *2015–2016 Managing Contraception: For Your Pocket.* Tiger, GA: Bridging the Gap Foundation, 2015. |

Index

CPSIA information can be obtained
at www.ICGtesting.com
Printed in the USA
FFOW05n1047151215